Sheikh Javed Usmani

An Investigation into the Negative Effects of Social Media

D1810796

Sheikh Javed Usmani

An Investigation into the Negative Effects of Social Media

Information Technology and Management GeoSpatial Technology

LAP LAMBERT Academic Publishing

Impressum / Imprint

Bibliografische Information der Deutschen Nationalbibliothek: Die Deutsche Nationalbibliothek verzeichnet diese Publikation in der Deutschen Nationalbibliografie; detaillierte bibliografische Daten sind im Internet über http://dnb.d-nb.de abrufbar.

Alle in diesem Buch genannten Marken und Produktnamen unterliegen warenzeichen-, marken- oder patentrechtlichem Schutz bzw. sind Warenzeichen oder eingetragene Warenzeichen der jeweiligen Inhaber. Die Wiedergabe von Marken, Produktnamen, Gebrauchsnamen, Handelsnamen, Warenbezeichnungen u.s.w. in diesem Werk berechtigt auch ohne besondere Kennzeichnung nicht zu der Annahme, dass solche Namen im Sinne der Warenzeichen- und Markenschutzgesetzgebung als frei zu betrachten wären und daher von jedermann benutzt werden dürften.

Bibliographic information published by the Deutsche Nationalbibliothek: The Deutsche Nationalbibliothek lists this publication in the Deutsche Nationalbibliografie; detailed bibliographic data are available in the Internet at http://dnb.d-nb.de.

Any brand names and product names mentioned in this book are subject to trademark, brand or patent protection and are trademarks or registered trademarks of their respective holders. The use of brand names, product names, common names, trade names, product descriptions etc. even without a particular marking in this work is in no way to be construed to mean that such names may be regarded as unrestricted in respect of trademark and brand protection legislation and could thus be used by anyone.

Coverbild / Cover image: www.ingimage.com

Verlag / Publisher:
LAP LAMBERT Academic Publishing
ist ein Imprint der / is a trademark of
OmniScriptum GmbH & Co. KG
Heinrich-Böcking-Str. 6-8, 66121 Saarbrücken, Deutschland / Germany
Email: info@lap-publishing.com

Herstellung: siehe letzte Seite /
Printed at: see last page
ISBN: 978-3-659-71527-3

Zugl. / Approved by: Nixon University

AN INVESTIGATION INTO THE NEGATIVE EFFECTS OF SOCIAL MEDIA AND CHALLENGES IT CREATES IN CRISES MANGEMEN

By

Dr. Sheikh Javed Usmani

PhD (Information Technology & Management)

MPhil (GeoInformatics (RemoteSensing / GIS))

MBA (Project management)

MSc-IT (Information Technology)

MCM (Information Technology & Management)

ACKNOWLEDGEMENT

First of all, it would give me great pleasure to show my gratitude to my professor, for his propositions, remarks, understanding and patience. It would also be an honour to express gratitude to my parents, my mother, my father, my sister and my brother for their endless support in my life and allowing me to make all my decisions. I would also like to take the opportunity to show appreciation to my co-workers for their expert cooperation on every occasion. I would also like to be grateful to the Department, managers of the university, instructors and students who have supported me throughout this research.

ABSTRACT

Similar to individuals using impression management to influence image, organizational impression management (OIM) suggests organizations use communications tactics to influence public opinion of company image and brand. OIM has been studied sporadically across industries and communications, but not within the field of law and sporadically across industries and communications, but not within the field of law and social media. The purpose of this causal comparative quantitative study was to examine if there were differences in social media OIM strategies based on financial performance and litigation specialty by the largest revenue-grossing U.S. law firms. Although law firms may be hesitant to use social media due to legal and ethical constraints, studies have shown increased use among them. This study analyzed nearly 10,000 Twitter messages posted by six purposefully selected law firms over a 5-year period. Diction software was used to measure five OIM metrics, represented in rhetorical tone, which showed higher- revenue law firms exhibited higher *Certainty* and *Optimism* than lower-revenue firms. Subsequent analysis through repeated measures ANOVA confirmed differences in *Certainty*, although not statistically significant (p = .063). There were no statistically significant differences among litigation specialties. There was a statistically significant difference in *Activity* between years 2011 and 2014 (p = .040), and a nearly significant difference between years 2010 and 2014 (p = .058). All firms over five years scored lower on *Certainty* and *Realism* than

Diction's normative range. This dissertation has added to OIM research by examining OIM strategies used in social media by the largest revenue-grossing U.S. Law firms.

Keywords: Organizational impression management, social media, brand image, OIM, Twitter, Facebook, Youtube

Table of Content

Chapter 1: Introduction to the Study 1

Introduction 1

Background of the Study 7

Problem Statement 13

Purpose of the Study 15

Research Questions 17

Advancing Scientific Knowledge 20

Significance of the Study 22

Rationale for Methodology 25

Nature of the Research Design for the Study 27

Definition of Terms 29

Impression management (IM). 29

Organizational impression management (OIM). 29

Anticipatory tactics. 29

Social networking. 30

Social media. 30

Legitimacy. 30

Initial public offering (IPO). 30

Corporate social responsibility (CSR). 31

Cause-related marketing (CRM). 31

Direct assertive OIM tactics. 32

Direct defensive OIM tactics. 32

Indirect OIM tactics. 32

Direct and indirect defensive OIM tactics. 32

Stakeholder. 32

Revenue-grossing. 32

Assumptions, Limitations, Delimitations 33

Summary and Organization of the Remainder of the Study 35

Chapter 2: Literature Review 37

Introduction to the Chapter and Background of the Problem 37

Theoretical Foundations 39

Review of the Literature 43

Historical foundations of impression management. 44

Individual IM within organizations. 46

Evolution to organizational impression management. 51

OIM and the legal industry. 93

Concluding remarks. 103

Summary 109

Chapter 3: Methodology 112

Introduction 112

Statement of the Problem 113

Research Question (s) and Hypotheses 115

Research Methodology 120

Research Design 121

Population and Sample Selection 124

    Population. 125

    Sample. 125

    Stratification. 127

    Exclusions. 129

    Initial review of public organizational web sites. 129

    Confidentiality measures. 130

Instrumentation 130

    Independent variables. 131

    Dependent variables. 132

    Measurement. 132

Validity 133

    Functional validation. 134

    Semantic validation. 135

    Sampling validity. 135

    Content validity 136

    Internal and external validity. 137

Reliability. 137

Stability.. 137

Replicability... 138

Accuracy... 138

Data Collection Procedures 139

Use of public data. 140

Procedure for identification/collection of social media data................ 140

Collection of organizational posts. 141

Data security. 143

Data Analysis Procedures... 144

Data.. 145

Preparation of data.. 146

Analysis of data. 149

Ethical Considerations 151

Limitations 152

Limitations with software.. 152

Limitations with content.. 152

Limitations of OIM variables. 153

Limitations of researcher analysis. 153

Summary 154

Chapter 4: Data Analysis and Results 157

Introduction... 157

Descriptive Data 160

Data Analysis Procedures 164

Preparation of data. 167

Rhetorical tone analysis through Diction. 168

Analysis of Diction scores. 170

Statistical analysis. 172

Validity and reliability. 172

Pilot study. 173

Summary 192

Chapter 5: Summary, Conclusions, and Recommendations 196

Introduction. 196

Summary of the Study 198

Summary of Findings and Conclusion 201

Alignment to OIM theory. 202

Analysis of Diction scores. 204

Inferences from statistical analysis. 210

Implications 219

Theoretical implications. 223

Practical implications. 224

Future implications. 225

Recommendations. 226

Recommendations for future research... 226

Recommendations for practice.. 228

References... 233

Appendix A. Data Analysis 253

Appendix B. Methodology of OIM Studies 255

Appendix C. Diction Variables... 258

Appendix D. OIM tied to Rhetorical Tone Variables 271

Appendix E. Research in Motion.. 275

List of Table

Table 1. Taxonomy of Organizational Impression Management Tactics 52

Table 2. Direct/Assertive Organizational Impression Management Tactics 53

Table 3 Direct/Defensive Organizational Impression Management Tactics 56

Table 4 Indirect Organizational Impression Management Tactics 59

Table 5. Social Media Use by Legal Firms on the AmLaw 100 List 128

Table 6. AmLaw 100 Firms with Designated Specialties using Social Media 161

Table 7. AmLaw 100 Firms with Social Media 162

Table 8. Criteria for Sample Selection 163

Table 9. Comparison of Normative Range for Diction Master Variables 177

Table 10. Collective Twitter Results Master Variables 178

Table 11. Distribution of Dependent Variables 182

Table 12. Comparison of Rhetorical Tone Between Upper and Lower-revenue Quartiles
.... 185

Table 13. Differences in Rhetorical Tone Among Specialty 188

Table 14. Comparison of Rhetorical Tone Over 5 Years 190

Chapter 1: Introduction to the Study

Introduction

"Contrary to what lawyers are fond of saying, documents never speak for themselves—interpretations are always made by intelligent readers. And texts inevitably have multiple meanings" (Krippendorff, 2013, p. 357). Readers work from within their own constructs, yet texts mean different things to different people. Analysts realize that how language is interpreted has much to do with the text writer, the audience, and the ways the writer endeavors to influence that audience.

The purpose of this causal comparative quantitative study was to examine if there were differences in social media organizational impression management (OIM) strategies based on financial performance and litigation specialty by the largest revenue-grossing U.S. law firms. This exploration can assist managers and researchers in understanding how financially successful organizations manage their brand impressions via social media. Rooted in dramaturgical and self-presentation social psychology theory, impression management (IM) was first introduced by Goffman (1959) as the process of creating, influencing, or manipulating an image held by an audience. Impression management occurs when individuals, as actors, attempt to control the impressions others form of them (Winter, Saunders, & Hart, 2003). Individuals, thus, behave in ways much like theatrical performances to influence the perceptions of their audience, portray themselves favorably, and minimize negative impressions.

Organizations, like individuals, are concerned with self-presentation of company image and brand. Two basic motives for engaging in OIM are desire for approval and desire for status (Highhouse, Brooks, & Gregarus, 2009). A third motive is to combat negative organizational image (Tyler, Connaughton, Desrayaud, & Fedesco, 2012). Organizations attempt to gain approval from the appropriate constituencies by projecting integrity and success. They also strive to gain status through admiration, prominence, and prestige (Highhouse et al., 2009). Industry rankings have become a status marker in recent years (McDonnell & King, 2013). Since organizations attempt to gain approval and status from their appropriate constituencies, one way to identify successful companies is through lists put out by those same constituencies, such as *Fortune 500, Fortune's Top 100 Employers to Work For, Most Admired Companies*, or industry lists of the largest revenue-producing firms (Highhouse et al., 2009; McDonnell & King, 2013). Accordingly, this study identified a stratified purposive sample of six firms from the 100 largest revenue-grossing law firms as named in the legal industry's 2013 *American Lawyer Magazine*.

Moreover, a review of the literature reveals OIM has not been studied as extensively as individual IM, especially in the use of social media as a platform (Bolino, Kacmar, Turnley, & Gilstrap, 2008). Exploration of OIM is lacking across industries, as researchers have indicated a need to further explore OIM in social media of various industries (Bolino et al., 2008; Doohwang, Hyuk Soo, & Jung Kyu, 2011; Jin & Lee, 2010; Kucuk, 2010; Lamertz & Martens, 2011; Schniederjans, Cao, & Schniederjans, 2013). Prior research revealed that organizations have used OIM strategies in the form of visual cues, such as graphs, pictures, web sites, as well as, verbal symbolism through semantics, rhetorical tone, and choice of verbiage in corporate narratives (Brennan, Guillamón-Saorín, & Pierce, 2008; Highhouse et al., 2009; Schniederjans et al., 2013). The primary channels for OIM strategies have traditionally been press releases, accounting narratives, and other forms of corporate communications (Brennan et al.,2008).

In contrast, social media is a decidedly different platform from traditional corporate communications due to its rapid availability, larger audience, and two-way communication capabilities. Consumers have embraced social media with a vengeance, yet companies are not fully utilizing its communication capabilities (Kwok & Yu, 2013). Greater exposure and visibility through social media can rapidly impact organizational image among various stakeholders, such as shareholders, clients, customers, employees, suppliers, government, media, and the community at large (Bolino et al. 2008; Patelli & Pedrini, 2013; Saxton & Guo, 2012; Schniederjans et al. 2013). An important area of future research is how successful organizations use OIM to "strategically position themselves in the eyes of their stakeholders" (Bolino et al., 2008, p. 1098). According to

Bolino et al. (2008), IM research at the organizational level has been limited, leaving the field "wide-open" (p. 1098). Much as others have studied *Fortune 500* companies because of their large revenues, this study has added to the research by exploring OIM strategies of the largest revenue-grossing law firms due to the influential role they play in the industry (Barnes, Lescault, & Wright, 2013). Organizational impression management is based on the view that both individuals and organizations share the same social objectives (Highhouse et al., 2009); therefore, an exploration of the organizational self-presentation motives of successful law firms can add to the body of knowledge of OIM across various industries.

Further, social media has changed the way organizations manage their image; thus, it is vital to understand how those in an industry bound by legal and ethical

constraints practice OIM via social media (Demay, 2011). The overall culture of law firms includes confidentiality, privacy, and conservatism, all of which directly conflict with the "disclosure culture" of social media (Vinson, 2010). For this reason, law firms have been hesitant to adopt the use of social media beyond company blogs. According to LexisNexis (2014b), Twitter and LinkedIn have been identified as the top social media choices of law firms. Benefits of social media include establishing expertise, attracting business, and gathering information (Vinson, 2010). However, ethical issues remain a major concern for law firms. For example, contact with witnesses, clients, adversaries, jurors, and others could violate discovery rules and have other ethical consequences. Ethical issues notwithstanding, there are legal consequences for violation of American Bar Association (ABA) rules.

Even with legal and ethical constraints, the legal industry has increased its use of social media, although many in the industry are still hesitant (Vinson, 2010). Social media was expected to grow to 1.43 billion users in 2013 (Schniederjans et al., 2013). Therefore, it is an important tool that organizations, and even entire industries, cannot afford to ignore. This exploration of OIM strategy used by successful law firms via social media may aid others in understanding how social media can be used to an organization's advantage.

At the same time, law firms must use marketing strategies that remain within legal and ethical guidelines, avoiding the violations that have plagued companies in other industries that have used social media for marketing. For example, the Federal Trade Commission (FTC) recently investigated Cole Haan fashion house for violation of advertising disclosure requirements on a social media site (Bobowski, 2014). The implication is that clever usage of OIM as a marketing tool can be used to persuade stakeholders to view the organization in a favorable light. In essence, law firm communications must reflect the legal constraints under which they operate (Krippendorff, 2013).

In summary, social media has changed the way organizations communicate with stakeholders and strategically manage their image (Hale, 2010). Those in the legal profession, as well as others marketing organizational attributes via social media, can heed information gleaned from a study of successful OIM strategy bound by these constraints. The remainder of Chapter 1 addresses the evolution of OIM theory from an individual perspective to organizational strategy. It identifies the problem statement of this study, along with the purpose statement and significance of the research. The research questions for the present study explored what OIM strategies are used by successful U.S. law firms in social media and examined differences based on revenue and litigation type. The latter part of the chapter briefly explains why quantitative methodology and a causal comparative research design, along with a content analysis data collection approach, were chosen for the analysis of social media. A stratified purposive sample was selected from the 100 largest revenue-grossing U.S. law firms as named in the *American Lawyer* magazine. The largest revenue-grossing law firms were chosen for this study precisely to explore the OIM strategies in social media of financially successful firms. Chapter 1 ends with a definition of terms used throughout the rest of the paper and considers any assumptions, limitations, or delimitations of the study.

Background of the Study

Impression management stems from dramaturgical self-presentation theory and is defined as the process by which an individual "actor" attempts to manipulate, influence, or maintain his or her image to others (Chilcutt, 2009). Goffman (1959) introduced this concept to explain the motivations behind human behavior in social settings. Jones and Pittman (1982) later applied IM theory to organizational behavior, with early studies done in the areas of interviewing, performance reviews, leadership, organizational commitment, organizational citizenship behaviors, and management (Bolino, 1999; Nagy, Kacmar, & Harris, 2011; Zinko, Furner, Royle, & Hall, 2010).

Jones and Pittman (1982) identified and categorized five measurable IM behaviors exhibited by individuals in organizational settings. These original IM behaviors lay the foundation for organizational IM behaviors: (a) Ingratiation involves the use of flattery and compliments to manipulate others in an organizational setting; (b) self- promotion involves highlighting accomplishments and bragging about one's competence; (c) exemplification involves volunteering and serving as a role model, especially for undesirable tasks; (d) intimidation is defined as a negative IM behavior since it involves bullying or intimidating others to alter the balance of power; and (e) supplication involves acting either helpless or incompetent to receive more help, training, or reduced workload (Jones & Pitman, 1982). The Jones-Pittman taxonomy has been used as the basis for individual IM behavior within organizational settings for several decades since its development (Mohamed, Gardner, & Paolillo, 1999).

Eventually, OIM developed to focus on organizational actors who attempt to control perceptions of their brands and organizational image (Doohwang et al., 2011).

The goal of the actor is to effectively manipulate impressions to the audience to achieve desired goals (Chilcutt, 2009). Organizational impression management studies have focused on marketing, brand awareness, and organizational defense tactics to combat negative publicity, maintain reputation, and manage stakeholder's perceptions (Chilcutt,2009; Lamertz & Martens, 2011; Nagy, Pollack, Rutherford, & Lohrke, 2012; Vlasic & Langer, 2012; Zeller, Stanko, & Jin, 2012). Prior studies used the OIM taxonomy developed by Mohamed et al. (1999) in which organizational behaviors, called *tactics*, were based upon Jones and Pittman's (1982) individual-behavior IM taxonomy. These tactics were broadly classified as direct assertive, indirect assertive, direct defensive, and indirect defensive (Mohamed et al., 1999). Organizations use assertive tactics to boost or improve their image through advertising, fundraisers, intimidation, organizational promotion, or cause-related marketing, among other communications (Patelli & Pedrini, 2013). Organizations, in turn, use defensive tactics to minimize damage or repair image through disclaimers, apologies, downplay of severity, restitution, or other pro-social behaviors

(Vielhaber & Waltman, 2008). In essence, organizations use assertive and defensive tactics much like individuals.

One problem in prior OIM research has been the variety of methods used (Bolino et al., 2008). Studies have ranged from qualitative research to mixed methods analysis (Brennan et al., 2008; Chilcutt, 2009; Pollach & Kerbler, 2011; Schniederjans et al.,2013). In addition, the Mohamed et al. (1999) taxonomy has been used in some studies but not in others, making it difficult to build upon and synthesize existing research (Bolino et al., 2008). However, the Mohamed et al. taxonomy laid the foundational categories for OIM research and has often been used as a classification tool for a variety of assertive and defensive behaviors. Still other researchers have tied OIM to a variety of organizational behaviors used to strategically manage image. For example, through text mining and other linguistic analysis methods, researchers have associated negative tone and use of personal pronouns to OIM defensive behaviors (Craig, Mortensen, & Iyer, 2013; Vielhaber & Waltman, 2008).

In other words, OIM behaviors extend beyond the Mohamed et al. (1999) taxonomy to include any communication that strategically creates, manages, or maintains image to an organziation's publics. According to Goffman's (1959) symbolic interactionist theory, organizations carefully construct images as do individuals. OIM strategies can be in the form of pictures, graphs, press releases, portrayals, web sites, letters, CEO profiles, or through any form of organizational communications as evidenced by the literature review. Since earlier research used traditional media communications, this study examined social media as the organizational communications vehicle. The OIM strategies were measured in rhetorical tone through content analysis of law firm's social media.

Therefore, the present study addressed deficiencies in OIM research. Prior literature reveals OIM has not been studied as extensively as individual IM and that research has been sporadic across industries, contexts, and methods. The first contribution of this study was to see if there are differences between OIM strategies used in social media and financial performance. "Corporations, like people, are concerned with "self-presentation'..." (Highhouse et al., 2009, p. 1483). Organizations, much like individuals, want to preserve and maintain their image to gain approval and status from their constituents. To reach these goals, many organizations use IM to get their names on lists of most coveted firms in an industry, such as *Fortune's* lists of the top revenue- producing firms (Bolino et al., 2008). The researcher used law firms named as the largest revenue grossing from the industry's annual list. The research questions for the current study explored what OIM strategies are used by successful U.S. law firms in social media and examined differences based on revenue and litigation type. The research questions are summarized in Appendix A.

Secondly, the researcher used social media as the platform for OIM strategies. Because of its popularity among law firms and for reasons stated in Chapter 2, social media in this study was confined to Twitter. Similar OIM research using the term *social media* has been confined to Facebook (Kwok, 2012). Social media is defined in the Definition of Terms, section and different types of social media are presented for a well- rounded discussion. Research at the organizational level has been limited to public reports, annual letters to shareholders, mass media, and other special company programs. The emergence of social media has allowed a new platform for organizations to diffuse information to stakeholders (Saxton & Guo, 2012; Schniederjans et al., 2013). Organizations have the ability to strategically share desired information with their publics, as well as attempt to control negative perceptions through social media. Because social media has changed the ways organizations communicate marketing efforts and attempt to manage brand perceptions (Kwok & Yu, 2013; Lovejoy, Waters, & Saxton,

2012), it may be useful to understand how this tool can be used to increase organizational presence, gain wider exposure to broad audiences, and clearly establish desired image (Hale, 2010).

Thirdly, this research study examined OIM strategies via social media used by successful law firms. In a meta-analysis of IM research, Bolino et al. (2008) determined that OIM studies in general are limited in scope and across industries. In addition, research has been limited to the study of written and verbal IM approach, with even fewer studies examining organization's electronic communications (Bolino et al., 2008). Though a handful of industries have been represented in prior studies, OIM via social media in the legal industry has not been researched. Other industries are underrepresented, but only the legal industry can offer insight into how OIM via social media can be used as a marketing tool within the constraints of legal and ethical guidelines of the legal profession. Understanding OIM strategies within an industry that has strict ethical and legal constraints (Lamertz & Martens, 2011) can offer valuable input into how successful firms manage their image. Marketers in other types of organizations need to be mindful of legal issues in advertising via social media by maintaining compliance with industry regulators and governing bodies such as the FTC (Bobowski, 2014).

In summary, the current study contributed to OIM research by examining OIM strategies used in a relatively new communications platform in an industry that has not been studied. This study addressed the corresponding problem statement: It is not known if there are differences in social media OIM strategies based on financial performance and litigation specialty by the largest revenue-grossing U.S. law firms. Increasing numbers of consumers and organizations search social media to find legal counsel, maintain informal contact, and look for guidelines when establishing their own social media policies (LexisNexis, 2014a). Solicitation of sophisticated legal advice is no longer reserved to traditional methods. As a result, legal and ethical compliance is of utmost importance to those in the legal industry (Vinson, 2010). Studying strategies of successful law firms may, therefore, assist other organizations with using social media as a marketing tool to enhance organizational image. With the popularity and importance of social media, research on how it is used to manage brand impressions is both timely and relevant (Hall, Pennington, & Lueders, 2013).

Problem Statement

It is not known if there are differences in social media OIM strategies based on financial performance and litigation specialty by the largest revenue-grossing U.S. law firms. Organizational impression management is often used to achieve status and approval among industry constituents, gain public trust, and manage brand image (Saxton & Guo, 2012). Organizational impression management research within social media is relatively limited and deficient within specific industries (Bolino et al., 2008). Therefore, this study added to the body of knowledge of OIM via social media within the legal industry.

Organizations, especially law firms, need to be cognizant of the impressions they convey with either presence or absence of particular content in their web sites, social media, press releases, annual reports, and other communications (Pollach & Kerbler, 2011; Saxton & Guo, 2012). Previously, organizations could control image and one-way messaging, but technology has facilitated two-way external communications (Vielhaber & Waltman, 2008). Social media has the ability to rapidly cause great harm, as well as great opportunity, because of instantaneous communications from a number of sources. For example, organizational stakeholders expect quick and easily available information in response to negative publicity or an organizational crisis (Vielhaber & Waltman, 2008). Because of this rapid dissemination of information, social media plays a disproportionate role in comparison to traditional communications platforms. The study of OIM via social media has important implications since gaining public trust is critical for most organizations (Tyler et al., 2012). Understanding how successful organizations deal with company image amid rapid, visible dissemination of communications can aid others in their marketing efforts. Thus, exploration of OIM strategies used by successful firms may be used as a benchmarking tool for organizations in formulating their social media strategies.

Specifically, exploration of OIM strategies can assist others in the legal industry in understanding how successful law firms use it for organizational advantage. Organizational impression management strategy plays a central role in formulating perceptions of company image and has particular significance for law firms that face challenges in a very competitive industry. A recent poll by LexisNexis (2014b) showed the tremendous impact of social media on the legal industry, ranging from solicitation of clients to various regulatory requirements. Law firms and legal professionals must be cognizant of the changes social media is necessitating in this traditional industry. Thus, those in the legal industry may find this study useful.

Another important consideration is that, since law firms are bound by legal and ethical constraints in their public communications, exploration of their OIM strategies may prove useful to organizations outside this population (Demay, 2011; Lamertz & Martens, 2011). Social media has brought changes to other industries as well, and rapid dissemination of information can be both advantageous and harmful. The understanding of how successful firms use OIM via social media within a highly regulated industry may assist others in formulating strategy. This knowledge may help marketers in other industries develop a set of best practices to improve or enhance public perceptions of company image.

Purpose of the Study

The purpose of this causal comparative quantitative study was to examine if there were differences in social media OIM strategies based on financial performance and litigation specialty by the largest revenue-grossing U.S. law firms. Content analysis has been successfully used in prior OIM studies and is an appropriate data collection technique for the purpose of this research (See Appendix B). The population under study is composed of 100 U.S. law firms named in the legal industry's 2013 *American Lawyer* annual list of largest revenue-grossing firms. A stratified purposive sample (Zhang & Wildemuth, 2009) of six law firms was selected from this population. Krippendorff (2013) defined *population* as the group central to the study and *stratified purposive sample* as the target group chosen to represent the population due to unique characteristics or criteria.

For the purposes of this study, the sample must have met several criteria. First, firms must have been U.S.-based. Secondly, they must have specialized in a litigation area rather than general litigation for objectivity into litigation type. Third, half of the sample was chosen from the top 25% and half from the bottom 25% for objectivity on financial ranking. Last, firms must have used social media. The litigation specialty and financial ranking criteria were added to represent and account for the strata, or subpopulations, within the general population (Krippendorff, 2013).

The independent variables were gross annual revenues of law firms, delineated as upper and lower quartiles of the *AmLaw 100* list, and litigation specialty type. The dependent variables were the OIM strategies measured by rhetorical tone of *Optimism, Certainty, Activity, Realism,* and *Commonality* used in social media by the largest revenue- grossing U.S. law firms. The five dependent variables were measured using an existing instrument and are further defined in Appendix C.

The main focus of this study stemmed from Goffman's (1959) IM theory. Impression management theory has roots in symbolic interactionism, which states that individuals try to manage the impressions others form of them

(Pollach & Kerbler, 2011). The IM social interaction model of individuals also encompasses how organizational actors tailor IM toward stakeholders. This manipulation was accomplished through dramatic enactment of public image (Lamertz & Martens, 2011). According to self- presentation theory, OIM is comprised of actions intentionally designed to influence stakeholders' perceptions (Bolino et al., 2008). Since financial performance is often an indication of successful firms, the current study examined the OIM strategies based on financial performance and litigation specialty type. This study examined what combination of the five OIM strategy metrics are used by successful firms.

Research Questions

The research questions for the current study explored what OIM strategies were used by successful U.S. law firms in social media and examined differences based on revenue and litigation type. The research questions were answered by exploring the OIM strategies of a purposive stratified sample of the largest revenue-grossing U.S. law firms. This may assist in understanding what OIM strategies are used by financially successful U.S. law firms to manage their brand impressions via social media. The following research questions and hypotheses guided this research study and address the stated problem:

R1: Do differences exist in any of the five OIM strategy metrics based on revenue

(bottom quartile versus top quartile)?

H1: At least one of the five OIM strategy metrics will be different based on revenue (bottom quartile versus top quartile).

H01: None of the five OIM strategy metrics will be different based on revenues (bottom quartile versus top quartile).

R2: Do differences exist in any of the five OIM strategy metrics based on specialty (labor law versus intellectual property versus product liability)? H2: At least one of the five OIM strategy metrics will be different based on specialty (labor law versus intellectual property versus product liability).

H02: None of the five OIM strategy metrics will be different based on specialty (labor law versus intellectual property versus product liability).

R3: Do differences exist in any of the five OIM strategy metrics based on year (2010 through 2014)?

H3: At least one of the five OIM strategy metrics will be different based on year (2010 through 2014).

H03: None of the five OIM strategy metrics will be different based on year (2010 through 2014).

The independent variables were gross annual revenues of law firms, delineated as upper and lower quartiles of the *AmLaw 100* list, and litigation specialty type. The dependent variables were the OIM strategies measured by rhetorical tone of *Optimism, Certainty, Activity, Realism,* and *Commonality* used in social media by the largest revenue-grossing U.S. law firms. The five dependent variables are defined in Chapters 2 and 3.

Advancing Scientific Knowledge

Impression management is defined as the process by which individual actors attempt to influence, manipulate, or control their impressions on others (Leary & Kowalski, 1990). Impression management stems from dramaturgical self-presentation and symbolic interactionist sociological theories (Schniederjans et al., 2013). Impression management theory regards individuals, teams, or even organizations as actors trying to achieve a means to an end through controlling image perception (Bolino et al., 2008). Impression management can be achieved through verbal communications, imaging, or even symbolic actions. Goffman (1959) theorized that individuals purposefully set out to maximize positive attributes and minimize negative qualities when forming impressions on others. The study of individuals in social and organizational settings has been researched extensively since Goffman first introduced IM theory. Though IM research has expanded to include organizational actors, studies of OIM are not widespread.

The study of OIM has important implications since gaining the support of stakeholders is critical for most organizations (Tyler et al., 2012). Company images are often conveyed via public communications, such as social media, press releases, and annual reports. Certain content in organizational communications can affect perceptions of company image (Pollach & Kerbler, 2011); therefore, it is important to understand which OIM strategies help improve company image. The continued study of OIM is important to organizational strategy and will contribute to OIM theory.

Furthermore, with the growing importance of social media, organizations must be cognizant of the messages they send (Parhankangas & Ehrlich, 2012).The literature has suggested that OIM strategies be explored across different types of organizations, industries, and communication methods (Avery & McKay, 2006; Bolino et al., 2008; Chilcutt, 2009; Tyler et al., 2012; Vielhaber & Waltman, 2008). Social media is still a relatively new communications platform and is lacking in OIM research (Demay, 2011). The study of OIM in different industries and communications platforms can have significant implications for organizational strategy (Osma & Guillamón-Saorín, 2009). Studies have identified the need for greater research across industries that have altogether different motives, goals, and stakeholders (O'Keefe & Conway, 2008). Scholars of OIM need to explore the role that organizational actors play in shaping institutional standards and the ways they carry out those projects (Lamertz & Martens, 2011). Therefore, the study of OIM via social media is both relevant and timely.

Examination of OIM strategy via social media in the legal field serves two areas of interest: (a) addressing the emergence of social media as a growing platform for organizational communications and (b) exploring OIM strategies of firms in an industry that is bound by legal and ethical constraints that somehow manage to be defined as "successful" through appearance on a coveted industry list. Legal industry culture is constrained by confidentiality agreements, privacy rules, and ethical conservatism, which, according to Vinson (2010), directly conflict with the highly public "disclosure Culture" of social media. Further, since law firms have to abide by ABA rules that restrict their marketing efforts, an exploration of their OIM strategies via social media can provide guidance to others in the legal industry. Additionally, this information can benefit marketers in other organizations that wish to expand the marketing capabilities of OIM while remaining within legal and ethical constraints of their own regulatory agencies. Overall, this research can help advance the study of OIM across industries and communications platforms.

Significance of the Study

Organizations are recognizing the growing impact social media has on brands and organizational image (Doohwang et al., 2011; Jin & Lee, 2010). From a research perspective, this study added to the body of knowledge on OIM strategy within social media. A limited amount of IM research exists at the organizational level, and it is specifically limited to a few industries and traditional communications methods (Bolino et al., 2008). With increasing reliance on technology, organizations need to understand how OIM strategies via social media can affect company image and brand. This study has important practical applications for organizations that wish to explore OIM strategies of successful firms within social media. Successful firms are often identified through financial rankings in industry lists (Highhouse et al., 2009; McDonnell & King, 2013).

As such, this study attempted to examine the OIM strategies in social media of successful firms based on financial revenues and litigation specialty type. Moreover, the study of OIM via social media is especially important for law firms because of the industry's ethical and legal limitations on public communications (Dayton, 2013). Many law firms do not engage in social media or do so sparingly since the industry has vague guidelines for this relatively new platform (Demay, 2011). Although law firms exhibit the first step of social domain parking (i.e., registering a name on a social media platform), many are still using social media as a one-way channel for corporate communications (LexisNexis, 2014b). The legal industry has experienced a decline in demand for legal services over recent years and has become a severely competitive industry (Press, 2013). Understanding how to effectively use this relatively new platform can be a source of competitive advantage.

To quote the legal database, LexisNexis (2014a), "Social media—two words that strike fear into the hearts of law firms partners… has most lawyers running for the hills" (p. 3). According to a recent poll by LexisNexis (2014a), smaller law firms are afraid of the legal implication of posting online, given all the regulations surrounding attorney- client privilege and unauthorized solicitations, among others. Larger firms are forced to use social media because of their size or vast geographical presence (LexisNexis, 2014a). Social media is a relatively new phenomenon, and studying the OIM strategies of successful firms can assist others.

Within the industry, prior IM studies in law have dealt with perceptions of courtroom behavior in settings where organizations were not able to manipulate controls (Miller, Wood, Sicafuse, & Chomos, 2010; Rose, Diamond, & Baker, 2010). However, information and image *can* be controlled in social media. Organizational impression management theory states that organizations manipulate information communicated to stakeholders in order to emphasize the positive and obfuscate the negative (Patelli & Pedrini, 2013). For example, Schniederjans et al. (2013) found a partial positive relationship between OIM strategy and financial performance, and other researchers have suggested that assertive OIM strategies can have positive effects on financial analyst's stock Recommendations (Pollach & Kerbler, 2011). Another study found that use of OIM strategies can affect a firm's initial public offering (IPO) (Lamertz & Martens, 2011).

Financial performance is often used as a mark of successful companies, and industry rankings have become a status marker in recent years (McDonnell & King, 2013). In fact, the 100 largest revenue-grossing firms billed more hours and pulled in higher fees than firms outside the *AmLaw 100* list, even as the economy slowed (Press, 2013). Based on prior studies that have used

Fortune's rankings and other industry rankings, this study's sample was taken from the 100 U.S. largest revenue-grossing law firms as named in *American Lawyer Magazine's AmLaw 100* (Bolino et al., 2008). This study contributed to OIM research by exploring strategies used in the "new marketing channel" of social media (Hale, 2010, p. 1) and follows a handful of other studies that have tied OIM strategies to financial performance (Du, Bhattacharya, & Sen, 2010; Lamertz & Martens, 2011; Parhankangas & Ehrlich, 2012; Patelli & Pedrini, 2013; Schniederjans et al., 2013; Tetlock, Saar-Tsechanshy, & Macskassy, 2008). The study of OIM via social media may assist the broader population of law firms, as well as other organizations, in understanding how financially successful firms manage their brand impressions to stakeholders (Patelli & Pedrini, 2013; Vielhaber & Waltman, 2008). This information can be valuable to researchers and managers in developing an OIM strategy via social media to manage organizational and brand image.

Rationale for Methodology

This study used a quantitative methodology, a causal comparative research design, with an historical content analysis data collection technique to examine the OIM strategies in social media based on financial performance and litigation specialty.

Quantitative studies use variables with numeric data for statistical analysis, such as annual gross revenues in the present study. Further, OIM strategies in law firm's social media were measured numerically through use of a validated measurement tool. Therefore, quantitative methodology was chosen to best assist in answering the research questions in this study. However, either qualitative, quantitative, or mixed-methods methodology has been used in recent OIM studies (Avery & McKay, 2006; Bravo, Matute, & Pina, 2012; Brennan et al., 2008; Chilcutt, 2009; Craig & Brennan, 2012; Hall et al., 2013; Lamertz & Martens, 2011; McDonnell & King, 2013; O'Keefe & Conway, 2008; Osma & Guillamón-Saorín, 2009; Patelli & Pedrini, 2013; Pollach & Kerbler, 2011; Schniederjans et al., 2013; Huang, Huang, Wu, & Hsieh, 2011; Tyler et al., 2012; Vielhaber & Waltman, 2008). A table of OIM studies with corresponding methodologies is shown in Appendix B.

Thus, the majority of prior OIM research has used quantitative and mixed-methods studies to systematically analyze descriptive output, such as word count, frequencies, semantics, rhetorical tone, and other quantifiable features of linguistics (Pollach & Kerbler, 2011). Whereas, qualitative OIM studies may begin with descriptive data (Bolino et al., 2008), they are better suited to studies seeking to explore and identify new themes or emerging patterns (Saldana, 2009). The current study needed a quantitative methodology utilizing causal comparative design to best examine OIM strategies in social media based on financial performance and litigation specialty.

In summary, the research questions for the present study were best answered through quantitative methodology. Law firm's OIM strategies were represented in numerical terms through use of a validated software tool, discussed in Chapter 3. Since the variables for this study were quantifiable, and the research questions required a causal comparative design, quantitative methodology was appropriate (Krippendorff, 2013). The intent of this study was to explore OIM strategies used by successful law firms via their social media and examine whether or not there are differences based on financial performance and litigation specialty type. The research questions were best answered through a quantitative methodology.

Nature of the Research Design for the Study

The present study used quantitative methodology, a causal comparative research design, with an historical content analysis data collection technique. The statistical analysis needed to answer the research questions required a causal comparative research design. The research questions asked for a comparison of differences of OIM strategies among firms based on revenue and litigation specialty. Causal comparative design is an explanatory correlational research design that best fit the needs of this study (Gravetter & Wallnau, 2013). In contrast, predictive correlational designs seek to identify a predictor variable to identify an outcome or make a forecast, which was not the goal of this study. Experimental studies, while quantitative, require manipulation of a variable in order to influence an outcome. The present study did not manipulate variables but was exploratory in nature. Thus, a causal comparative design was chosen over other quantitative methods.

In summary, this study utilized a causal comparative design, since the intent was to examine the OIM strategies via social media based on financial performance and litigation specialty (Krippendorff, 2013; Neuendorf, 2002). The present study examined the largest U.S. revenue-grossing law firms from the industry's *AmLaw 100* list. A purposive sample was taken from the list to represent firms that are U.S.-based and specifically used Twitter; however, the researcher noted the use of organizational blogs and LinkedIn for the purpose of choosing firms that are active in social media. To represent the strata, or subpopulations, firms that specialized in different types of litigation were used to account for sub-population differences. For financial objectivity, each half of the sample was chosen from the upper and lower quartiles in financial ranking (Krippendorff, 2013). Six firms were chosen that fit the selection criteria. Thus, a causal comparative design was appropriate to examine the OIM strategies of the sample. The following section defines the terms that are used operationally for this study.

Definition of Terms

The following terms were used operationally in this study.

Impression management (IM). Impression management includes efforts by a person to create, maintain, protect, or alter an image held by others to influence control of information and create desired image (Schniederjans et al., 2013).

Organizational impression management (OIM). Just as individuals are social actors, so are organizations concerned with image and self-presentation (Highhouse et al., 2009). The conveyance of images can come though annual reports, press releases, advertising, web sites, and other public vehicles aimed at various stakeholders (Tyler et al., 2012). Organizations maintain and establish impressions that they wish to convey to the public, making perception a reality (Chilcutt, 2009). Organizational impression management efforts are often used to generate legitimacy among various audiences (Lamertz & Martens, 2011).

Anticipatory tactics. The use of tactics with the goal of remedial OIM efforts following a publicly negative event or prevention of challenge or negative outcry (Tyler et al., 2012).

Social networking. The strategic use of web sites, blogs, and other electronic communications as marketing tools to connect with related audiences, establish roles, increase online presence, and promote success (Hale, 2010). *Social networking* is also referred to as Web 2.0 and can be done on organizational web sites, company blogs, LinkedIn, Twitter, Facebook, or any number of Web 2.0 sites. Dissemination of information via social networking on social media sites is often instantaneous and rapid.

Social media. Any Web 2.0 platform that has the ability to transmit mass communications among organizations, consumers, or any combination thereof (Hale, 2010), including company web pages, blogs, LinkedIn, Twitter, Google Plus, YouTube, Facebook, and a myriad of other emerging sites (Vinson, 2010). The term *social media* has commonly and generally been used throughout the literature to represent one or more Web 2.0 mass communications platforms.

Legitimacy. Obtaining favorable judgments of acceptance, appropriateness, viability, and worthiness about an individual or an organization, often tied to organizational behaviors (Nagy et al., 2012). Legitimacy is achieved through reputation, status, and an image of integrity (McDonnell & King, 2012).

Initial public offering (IPO). Entrance of a company into the public stock market. This process consists of actively engaging with a network of investment banks, lawyers, and accountants and publishing a prospectus document that outlines how the company intends to meet stakeholder's needs (Lamertz & Martens, 2011). The prospectus is a symbolic account of how the company wishes to portray itself.

Corporate social responsibility (CSR). Proactive and voluntary behavior of organizations beyond economic, ethical, and legal responsibilities. Examples of CSR activities are charitable or other philanthropic donations, contributions to causes, contribution of resources, or environmentally conscious behavior that benefits society as a whole (Du et al., 2010). Organizations engage in CSR activities to construct desired identities, manage external impressions, and legitimize behaviors to stakeholders (Bravo et al., 2012). These activities can be developed altruistically or for self-interest.

Cause-related marketing (CRM). CRM is closely related to CSR activities but usually are tied to direct causes or social issues. The active engagement of the organization ties it to the cause, thus becoming part of its image. CRM can be a challenge, especially if stakeholders suspect that commitment to social causes and CSR motives are communicated solely for intrinsic purposes (Du et al., 2010).

Direct assertive OIM tactics. These include ingratiation, intimidation, organizational promotion, exemplification, and supplication (Mohamed et al., 1999).

Direct defensive OIM tactics. These include accounts, disclaimers, organizational handicapping, apologies, restitution, and pro-social behavior (Mohamed et al., 1999).

Indirect OIM tactics. These include boasting, blaring, burnishing, and blasting (Mohamed et al., 1999).

Direct and indirect defensive OIM tactics. These include burying, blurring, boosting, and belittling (Mohamed et al., 1999).

Stakeholder. Anyone who has an interest in the organization, such as shareholders, clients, customers, employees, government, media, and the community (Bolino et al., 2008; Patelli & Pedrini, 2013; Schniederjans et al., 2013).

Revenue-grossing. Gross billings to clients (American Lawyer, 2013). Specific to this study, *American Lawyer Magazine* gross revenue rankings are based on fee income from legal work only. Gross revenue rankings exclude disbursements and income from nonlegal ancillary businesses (Press, 2013).

Assumptions, Limitations, Delimitations

Several assumptions were present in this study. First, it was assumed that the content analysis performed adequately identified OIM strategies. The use of content analysis software can be more subjective than hand coding (Krippendorff, 2013). It was expected that the dictionaries and subsequent editing of dictionaries provided a basis for the OIM categories. The drawback is that computer coding is sometimes not as accurate as hand-coding (Brennan et al., 2008) since computer coding cannot pick up the subtleties and nuances that manual coding can provide (Krippendorff, 2013). However, computer coding is more objective and consistent than manual coding.

Second, it was assumed that the largest revenue-producing firms in the U.S. are listed accurately in the top 100 list provided by *American Lawyer Magazine* each year. The firms listed in 2013 were named from the prior year. Therefore, this study identified firms in the top 100 two years prior to this writing. In difficult, volatile economic times, these rankings can change rapidly.

Several limitations/delimitations may be present in this study. This study was limited to U.S. law firms and did not consider the rankings of global firms. This study was further limited to the exploration of OIM strategies based on rhetorical tone from the data used in this study. Rhetorical tone may or may not accurately represent the sentiment conveyed through organizational communications through social media. For example, Twitter data is limited to 140 characters. It was assumed that a substantial number of "tweets" were downloaded to capture the rhetorical tone of the messages. In examining rhetorical tone through five variables, this study may have failed to acknowledge other variables or categorical taxonomies of equal importance. Though OIM strategies are not bound by any categorical framework, this study attempted to associate rhetorical tone to the Mohamed et al. (1999) taxonomy, as other researchers have attempted to do, without regard for other OIM taxonomies that may exist.

Lastly, in the interest of time constraints, this study explored the social media of a stratified purposive sample of the largest revenue-grossing U.S. law firms, not the list in its entirety. Additionally, legally regulated content, such as legal communications or those that can be construed as legal communications, reflect the constraints of the particular group. This may have presented a problem in extracting OIM themes from law firm's social media sites. The OIM themes may be hidden or latent as compared to more obvious and manifest content from other types of organizations.

Summary and Organization of the Remainder of the Study

Since Goffman (1959) first introduced the theory, IM of individuals has been studied extensively in both social and organizational settings. However, OIM, the process by which organizations attempt to control perceptions of their brands and organizational image, is still a relatively new field (Doohwang et al., 2011). A meta-analysis of OIM identified a need for more research on the study of organizational IM strategies (Bolino et al., 2008). Areas lacking include social media as a platform and exploration of OIM strategy of successful organizations across industries (Bolino et al., 2008; Doohwang et al., 2011; Jin & Lee, 2010; Kucuk, 2010; Lamertz & Martens, 2011; Schniederjans et al., 2013).

The current study has contributed to the growing body of knowledge regarding OIM, specifically via social media. The intended contribution was insight into what OIM strategies are used in social media by successful organizations based on financial performance and litigation specialty type. It is important for anagers to understand how successful organizations use OIM to "strategically position themselves in the eyes of their stakeholders" (Bolino et al., 2008, p. 1098). "Successful organizations" can be identified through lists such as *Fortune 500* (Bolino et al., 2008). In keeping with this definition, this study analyzed a sample from the largest 100 revenue-producing law firms as named in the 2013 *American Lawyer Magazine*. Few studies have attempted to link OIM strategies to financial performance

(Schniederjans et al., 2013). In particular, studies of successful law firms and their OIM strategies via social media have not been done.

Therefore, the current study used a quantitative methodology with a causal comparative design. An historical content analysis data collection technique was used to examine the OIM strategies in social media based on annual gross revenues and specialty type of successful U.S. law firms. A quantitative methodology was best to answer the research questions. The remainder of this document is organized as follows. Chapter 2 presents a literature review on the topic of IM and its evolution over the years. It will review OIM studies through various organizational objectives and image management strategies that have evolved from Goffman's (1959) IM theory. The literature review will describe OIM studies that have been done through traditional communications channels, such as press releases, and present the importance of social media as an influential marketing channel for OIM. Chapter 3 describes the methodology, research design, and procedures for this investigation. Chapter 4 details how the data was analyzed with both written and graphic summaries of the results. Chapter 5 will provide an interpretation and discussion of results.

Chapter 2: Literature Review

Introduction to the Chapter and Background of the Problem

Impression management has been studied extensively since Goffman (1959) introduced the theory that individual actors create, manipulate, and try to maintain their image to others. How individuals control and manipulate their image to others is rooted in dramaturgical theory (Goffman, 1959) and symbolic interactionist sociology theory (Schniederjans et al., 2013). In business settings, IM has been studied in situations such as employment interviews and leadership (Mohamed et al., 1999). Later, this theory evolved into OIM, whereby organizational actors strategically try to influence public perceptions to their advantage (Patelli & Pedrini, 2013). Public communications can help an organization manage, protect, maintain, and enhance its image (Chilcutt, 2009).

However, OIM via social media and the processes by which organizations attempt to control perceptions of their brands and image is still a relatively new field (Doohwang et al., 2011). Several OIM studies have used the taxonomy developed by Mohamed et al. (1999). Content analysis has been used to extract themes that correspond with the taxonomy's assertive and defensive tactics categories in a variety of studies (Avery & McKay, 2006; Bolino et al., 2008; Chilcutt, 2009; Parhankangas & Ehrlich, 2012; Tyler et al., 2012; Vielhaber & Waltman, 2008). However, deficient areas include OIM research in social media of successful organizations across different industries. The legal industry especially has been slow to adopt social media (Dayton, 2013).

The current study adds to the growing body of knowledge regarding OIM strategy via social media specifically within the legal industry, which was chosen for this study because it is uniquely constrained by legal and ethical guidelines. As such, an exploration of OIM tactics of successful law firms via their social media may provide guidance and insight to others regarding how successful firms use OIM for organizational advantage. Chapter 2 begins with a discussion of Goffman's theory of impression management to present historical and theoretical foundations for this study.

Thereafter, the following themes serve as the outline for the literature review section. The chapter covers the progression of individual IM studies within organizations, to organizational OIM studies over the past three decades. The OIM behaviors studied through traditional platforms have included corporate social responsibility campaigns (Brennan, Merkl-Davies, & Beelitz, 2013; Tyler et al., 2012), cause-related marketing (Doohwang et al., 2011), brand image and damage control (Chilcutt, 2009), and reputation management (Craig & Brennan, 2012). The chapter concludes with a discussion of OIM studies via social media, and how social media has changed the landscape for law firms.

Theoretical Foundations

This dissertation investigated the concept of OIM and the ways organizations attempt to carefully construct their public image. Rooted in dramaturgical self- presentation theory and symbolic interactionist theory, IM began in the fields of sociology and psychology as a study of individual behavior in social settings. *Impression management* is defined as the process by which an individual attempts to influence, manipulate, or control the impressions others form of them (Goffman, 1959).

Sociologist Goffman (1959) was the first to study IM behaviors of individuals and is considered the founder of social influence theory. Reflecting dramaturgical and self- presentation theory, Goffman, in his book *The Presentation of Self in Everyday Life,* referred to individuals as actors playing out their roles in a calculating manner to influence impressions on others and attempt to control situations. Innuendos, omissions, ambiguities, and other communication techniques allow the performer to present him or herself in a favourable light. According to Goffman, mass media and the American legal system have their own version of this manipulation, such that image influence, or even outright misrepresentation, can arise from words, omissions, ambiguous statements, nondisclosure, or prevention of discovery.

Hence, individuals offer two differing versions of expressiveness: those given through verbal symbols to deliver communications, and symbolic expressions that are intentionally meant to convey a certain expression to control other's perceptions or "inferences" of them and the situation (Goffman, 1959, p. 3). Sometimes these actions are highly calculated, and at other times, the individual will be unaware that he is conducting them in a particular manner. Oftentimes, an individual's role will lend him to unconsciously behave or react in a certain way. The public demands that individuals in particular professions conduct themselves in a certain manner, such that they do not stray from their role (Goffman, 1959). Goffman further contended that in everyday life, individual "performers" are very adept at creating false impressions without placing themselves in the "indefensible position of having told a clear-cut lie" (Goffman, 1959, p.62).

Thus, miscommunicative performances can be in the form of ambiguities, innuendos, and critical omissions that are just shy of outright untruths (Goffman, 1959). Goffman stated that regulatory agencies, such as those governing the real estate industry, often develop ethics codes, "specifying the degree to which doubtful impressions can be given by overstatement, understatement, and omissions" (Goffman, 1959, p. 62). Goffman further identified the legal aspects of misrepresentation as an intentional act meant to deceive others. Misrepresentation can arise from ambiguous verbiage as well as from non-disclosure of information.

More importantly, Goffman (1959) surmised that projected image in a given situation was fostered and sustained by a cooperation of several individuals. The second chapter of *The Presentation of Self in Everyday Life* covered Goffman's view on teamwork in organizations. He used examples of informality among coworkers ("Mary" and "Bob") that quickly change to formal relationships ("Dr. Jones" and "Mr. Smith") when outsiders are present. He coined the term *performance team* to reflect the cooperation among two or more performers that work together to project a certain image (Goffman, 1959). Thus, his work suggested teams engage in "theatrical performances" of image management not only for themselves, but to present a front for an organization (Goffman, 1959, p. 77).

Furthermore, Goffman's (1959) discussion of teamwork led to his speculation of organizational strategies. He firstly considered organizational "dark secrets," akin to those of intentional misrepresentation. These are secrets that could never be openly admitted to organizational publics. Secondly, he discussed "strategic secrets," which are commonly used in commercial communications to outmaneuver the opposition (Goffman, 1959, p. 142). Disclosure of strategic secrets, while not fatal to the organization, was still considered disruptive of team performance. Thirdly, he addressed "inside" secrets. Inside secrets were defined as those "whose possession marks an individual as being a member of a group and helps the group feel separate and different"(Goffman, 1959, p. 142). Inside secrets hold little importance in terms of strategy, but may make insiders feel "in the know'' at the exclusion of those on the outside. Goffman (1959) used lawyers in his example of disclosing client improprieties. In such a case, the lawyer's trustworthiness to his client is threatened and his client's show of innocence to the court is also threatened.

Accordingly, organizational actors must learn to perform their given roles. Dramaturgical performers learn to perform their "part" per expectations of others, without betraying their feelings. In individuals, this translates into the "management of one's face and voice" (Goffman, 1959, p. 217). For organizations, this means concentration on relaying a consistent message and effectively managing situations. Goffman (1959) concluded with the revelation that his analogy of performers and audiences was in part a rhetorical maneuver. Nonetheless, he stressed the importance of social encounters, maintenance of a situation among disruptions, and successful staging using "real" techniques—the same techniques by which everyday persons sustain their real social situations (Goffman, 1959, p. 255).

Hence, through OIM theory, organizations, not individuals, are viewed as manipulative actors who strategically undertake actions to influence organizational image (Bolino et al., 2008; Goffman, 1959; Vielhaber & Waltman, 2008). Consequently, organizations can apply OIM strategies to create and maintain positive image and minimize negative identity. Goffman's theories have appeared as the foundational work in a number of OIM studies, and served as the basis for the research by Rose et al.

(2010), entitled, *Goffman on the Jury: Real Jurors' Attention to the "Offstage" of Trials,* and more recently, Zavattaro's (2013), *Expanding Goffman's Theater Metaphor to an Identity-Based View of Place Branding.* A review of current literature reveals that OIM has evolved to become an important addition to organizational image management and marketing. Indeed, an Internet search on Google Scholar revealed that *The Presentation of Self in Everyday Life* has been cited 32,313 times at this writing.

In conclusion, the present quantitative study, utilizing causal comparative design, attempted to examine OIM strategies in social media based on financial performance and litigation specialty. It answered the research questions regarding differences in OIM strategy, as measured by rhetorical tone, based on annual gross revenues and specialty type among U.S. law firms. Although other industries are underrepresented in OIM research via social media, the legal industry is especially intriguing because law firms must utilize marketing strategies that remain within legal and ethical constraints. Thus, understanding how the largest revenue-grossing law firms use OIM via social media tools can offer essential insights for providing education and benchmarking for others in the legal industry (Alvarez, Dalton, Lamport, & Tsamis, 2014; Bobowski, 2014). The remainder of this chapter provides an overview of how OIM research has developed from Goffman's (1959) theories.

Review of the Literature

Organizational impression management has been defined as purposely crafting a public image to manage perceptions, combat negative images, and create a favorable image with a variety of stakeholders (Bolino et al., 2008; Chilcutt, 2009; Schniederjans et al., 2013). The use of OIM in marketing and public relations is pervasive and includes positioning, differential advantage, raising brand awareness, driving traffic, creating virtual buzz, and building brand equity (Chilcutt, 2009). The literature review begins with historical foundations of IM research and how it moved from social settings to the study of individuals within organizations. The chapter discussion progresses to show how OIM has been used in a variety of marketing campaigns to formulate brand and organizational image. While the majority of OIM studies have been done on traditional communications vehicles, the conclusion of the literature review covers recent studies that have used social media as an OIM strategic tool.

Historical foundations of impression management. As previously stated, IM is the process by which someone attempts to influence his or her image to others by manipulating the way others perceive him or her (Carlson, Carlson, & Ferguson, 2010; Turnley & Bolino, 2001). Goffman's (1959) theories of human interaction and symbolic interactionist theory gained popularity with the socio-psychological community.

Impression management theory was later adopted by organizational researchers who attempted to explain individual behavior in the workplace

(Leary & Kowalski, 1990). Since the concept was introduced to business in 1982, several studies have been done on IM in the workplace, notably involving employee-management issues (Nagy et al., 2011). An early influential work was Bolino's (1999) "Citizenship and Impression Management: Good Soldiers or Good Actors?" which focused on employee behaviors in organizational settings. Bolino's work has since inspired others in researching IM in organizations. Individual IM behaviors have been studied in marketing, organizations, and social situations. Jones and Pittman (1982) identified and categorized five measurable IM behaviors exhibited by individuals in organizational settings. The Jones-Pittman taxonomy has been used as the basis for individual IM behavior within organizational settings for several decades (Mohamed et al., 1999). The individual IM scale was used as recently as 2013 in a job satisfaction study conducted by Harris, Gallagher, and Rossi (2013).

The five original IM behaviors by Jones and Pittman (1982)—(a) ingratiation, (b) supplication, (c) exemplification, (d) intimidation, and (e) self-promotion—lay the foundation for organizational IM behaviors. Ingratiation involves the use of flattery and compliments to manipulate others in an organizational setting (Bolino & Turnley, 1999). Self-promotion tactics involve highlighting accomplishments and bragging about one's competence (Jones & Pitman, 1982). Exemplification involves volunteering and serving as a role model, especially for undesirable tasks (Harris et al., 2013). Exemplification is also used as a socially visible platform, with the goal of showing others the lengths to which the employee will go for the good of the organization, such as arriving at work early, helping struggling coworkers, or attending optional meetings to appear dedicated (Zinko et al., 2010). Intimidation is a negative IM behavior, since it involves bullying or intimidating others, whereby the employee utilizes force to alter the balance of power (Nagy et al., 2011). Lastly, supplication tactics involve acting either helpless or incompetent in order to receive more help, training, or reduced workload (Jones & Pitman, 1982).

Bolino and Turnley (1999) later developed an employee IM scale based on the five categories developed by Jones and Pittman (1982). The resulting scale contained 22 items related to the five tactics and was found to be a valid, reliable measurement tool of IM behaviors. The studies by Bolino and Turnley were replicated and the scale validated by Kacmar, Nagy, and Harris in 2007. This scale laid the foundation for future research, and the five categories have been used consistently in IM studies (Carlson et al., 2011; Nagy et al., 2011; Pandey, 1981; Yun, Takeuchi, & Liu, 2007; Zinko et al., 2010). The following sections highlight the progression of IM theory into OIM to provide a thorough understanding of the background concepts in this study.

Individual IM within organizations. Impression management behaviors that have been studied in the workplace include those that influence managerial outcomes in terms of interviews, hiring, promotions, performance appraisals, feedback-seeking, and leadership. Of the five IM categories, ingratiation and self-promotion have been the two most researched (Bolino et al., 2008; Turnley & Bolino, 2001). In an early study, Pandey (1981) explored how managers are influenced by ingratiation and concluded that ingratiators set out to control their superiors and have the power to influence managerial decisions. "Thus, ingratiation seems to function like counterfeit coins or coins of a wrong denomination used to cheat the slot machine to receive the pay-offs" (Pandey, 1981, p.67).

Impression management studies expanded to include other variables. Zinko et al. (2010) extended the study of IM behavior to include self-image and organizational citizenship behaviors (OCB). Organizational citizenship behaviors are identified when an employee plays the role of the "good soldier" (Bolino, 1999, p. 82) by volunteering for unwanted tasks, acting as role model, or applying for highly visible positions. The study by Zinko et al. sought to examine OCBs in light of how individuals view themselves and their organizational relationships, as well as associated IM tactics. They surveyed 199 employees in the U.S. and 84 in China and found that individuals perform OCBs to be rewarded but mostly to gain a favorable impression (Zinko et al., 2010). Yun et al. (2007) also established a link between OCBs and IM in the workplace: OCBs tend to have a positive effect on employer reward recommendations, much like the ingratiatory tactic of IM theory. Likewise, Nagy et al. (2011) conducted a study of 144 state workers to see if four personality variables (i.e., self-efficacy, self-esteem, neuroticism, and locus of control) had an effect on the five categories of IM behaviors in the workplace. They found that workers with higher scores on the four personality variables engaged less in IM behaviors than individuals who scored low. Those with overall low self-worth were more likely to engage in IM tactics (Nagy et al., 2011).

Impressions management expanded to leader-member exchange (LMX) theory, which is the study of relationships among managers and their employees (Carlson et al., 2011). Some of these exchanges involve the use of negative IM behaviors, defined as the two categories of supplication and intimidation. Examples of supplication are self- depreciating, appearing incompetent, saying things negatively, and behaving contrary to the norm to avoid unwanted tasks or to gain another desired outcome. Examples of intimidation include bullying and aggressive behavior. Carlson et al. (2011) surveyed 65 state government supervisors to measure the degree to which a subordinate was using deceptive IM behaviors and the ways these behaviors affected LMX. They found the use of negative IM behavior backfired when the intended target of the behavior, the supervisor, recognized the manipulation tactics and, thus, felt less favorably toward the employee. This outcome has been termed the *receiver's dilemma* by Gurevitch (1985), who studied the responses of recipients of IM behaviors. Although the receiver of the IM behaviors may have gained a favorable impression of the employee, the manipulation factor of the employee's behavior was repulsive. This finding mirrored early studies on negative IM behavior (Becker & Martin,

1995; Gurevitch, 1985). Ward and Brenner (2006) found that employees occasionally engage in negative acknowledgment, offer a disclaimer, or admit fault in order to improve an evaluation from another. Those who bring forth a negative property, such as admitting to unpreparedness, poor English skills, or lack of writing skills, before an event or evaluation can manipulate the outcome. The researchers concluded that if an action were prefaced with a negative statement, that it was evaluated less negatively than if it were not brought to light (Ward & Brenner, 2006).

More recently, research has been done on the impressions created by appearance. One study looked at strategic forms of sexuality in the workplace (Baskerville Watkins, Smith, & Aquino, 2013) and another at dress, such as casual, formal business, or business casual (Karl, McIntyre Hall, & Peluchette, 2013). Baskerville et al. (2013) focused on using sexuality as social influence in the workplace, through forms of dress, flirtation, compliments, and other gestures, to achieve desired ends. The researchers found that strategic sexual performance can be a tool to further employee's own interests and influence others. However, strategic sexual performance was sometimes ineffective (Baskerville et al., 2013). For example, ingratiation in the form of compliments is an IM tactic that can cause backlash if the compliments are perceived as dishonest and insincere by the receiver. Likewise, workplace attire was the IM context in a study by Karl et al. (2013) of working sector professionals in a variety of public occupations. Attire affected not only the perceptions that others formed of the individual employee but also self- perceptions and self-esteem (Karl et al., 2013), suggesting a connection between employee dress and consumer perceptions of service quality and organizational image.

Lastly, individual IM has been studied in the context of job satisfaction and career-related consequences. Harris et al. (2013) examined the relationships among workplace cultural IM norms and employee job satisfaction, strain, and burnout. Using the Jones and Pittman (1982) IM scale, Harris et al.found that certain tactics prevalent in the workplace and acceptance by some cultures were likely to be associated with either positive or negative outcomes (Harris et al., 2013). In sum, most IM studies in the workplace have focused on individuals within the organization.

Other types of IM studies considered consumer perceptions of individual self- image that they gleaned from brand usage. For example, Ferraro, Kirmani, and Matherly (2013) researched conspicuous brand usage by individuals who had strong identification connections to a particular brand. The purpose of conspicuous usage was to impress others through blatant flaunting of the product or brand name. Their finding was that people tend to view conspicuous brand behavior in a negative light. They also concluded that the brand should have a distinct and positive image for consumers to engage in IM behaviors (Ferraro et al., 2013). The study did not address brands that were not well- defined or well-known, yet the study of consumer behavior of this nature ties into the study of IM. Thus, the individual remained the IM focus in early brand studies.

Studies of individuals at the organizational level have been the most pervasive among IM research. Impression management studies of individuals have evolved from social situations to organizational settings in the past two decades. Goffman (1959) likened individual performers to actors attempting to influence an audience. In his seminal work *The Presentation of Self in Everyday Life*, Goffman included self- presentation behaviors of teams and organizational performers. Eventually, researchers began to look beyond individual IM behaviors and apply Goffman's theories to team situations. More importantly, IM research began to shift from the study of individuals to organizations in the past few years.

Evolution to organizational impression management. Impression management eventually evolved from the micro individual perspective to the macro-organizational level. Impression management consists of behaviors, symbolism, cues, or communications an individual projects to an audience to manage self-image. Some of these behaviors were systematically categorized into the Jones and Pittman (1982) taxonomy. The taxonomy of the original five individual IM behaviors by Jones and Pittman (1982) was revised by other researchers in 1985 (Chilcutt, 2009). The individual taxonomy was later translated into an OIM scale developed by Mohamed et al. (1999), who revised the individual scale to fit the organizational level; thus, organizations can be classified as ego-defensive, manipulative, and self-serving by engaging in IM behaviors. The resulting 2 x 2 OIM taxonomy had four main categories—(a) direct, (b) indirect, (c) assertive, or (d) defensive—without being mutually exclusive (Mohamed et al., 1999). The OIM taxonomy has been used as a categorical tool in several studies. Yet, some researchers have explored OIM behaviors without it. Much as the Jones-Pittman (1982) taxonomy did not capture all impression management behaviors, the OIM taxonomy may not accurately reflect the myriad of OIM behaviors. Although other OIM taxonomies may exist, this one in particular has been mentioned in the literature and its significance warrants mention in this study. The taxonomy of OIM tactics is shown in Table 1.

Table 1. Taxonomy of Organizational Impression Management Tactics

	Direct Tactics	Indirect Tactics
Assertive Tactics	Ingratiation Intimidation	Boasting
	Organizational promotion	Blaring
	Exemplification	Burnishing
Defensive Tactics	Accounts Disclaimers	Burying
	Organizational	Blurring
	handicapping	Boosting
	Apologies	Belittling
	Restitution	
	Pro-social behavior	

Moreover, the OIM taxonomy defined *organizational behaviors* as strategic tactics. The first distinction is whether the tactic is direct or indirect. Direct tactics involve purposeful manipulation, while indirect tactics attempt to manage associations with other entities for maintaining the desired image (Schniederjans et al., 2013). Both the direct and indirect categories were further broken down into assertive or defensive strategies. Direct/assertive tactics at the organizational level include ingratiation, intimidation, organizational promotion, exemplification, and supplication. The tactics listed in Table 2 are meant to create and augment a desirable image to an organization's target audience. Direct/defensive tactics are meant to protect organizational image or minimize negative repercussions or atone for transgressions (Mohamed et al., 1999). These tactics include accounts, disclaimers, organizational handicapping, apologies, restitution, and pro-social behavior. The taxonomy of all direct/defensive tactics is listed in Table 3. Table 4 lists all the indirect tactics that an organization may use to augment image. This scale has been used in prior OIM research either in whole or in part (Bolino et al., 2008; Chilcutt, 2009; Schniederjans et al., 2013; Vielhaber & Waltman, 2008).

Table 2. Direct/Assertive Organizational Impression Management Tactics

Behavior	Definition/Description	Example
Ingratiation	Behaviors that are used by organizational actors to make the organization appear more attractive to others.	Promotional campaigns by the armed services that portray a branch of the military as providing attractive career opportunities.
Intimidation	Behaviors that present the organization as a powerful and dangerous entity that is able and willing to inflict harm on those that frustrate its efforts and objectives.	A large manufacturer that threatens a small supplier with a reduction of orders unless it terminates its relationship with one of the firm's competitors.
Organizational promotion	Behaviors that present the organization as being highly competent, effective, and successful.	An organization that attributes the henomenal sales of a new product to its savvy marketing campaign.

Exemplification	Behaviors that are used by the organization to project images of integrity, social responsibility, and moral worthiness; this tactic may also have a goal of seeking imitation by other entities.	Fund-raising campaigns by the United Way that highlight the moral worthiness and social benefits that accrue from the charitable causes the organization supports.
Supplication	Behaviors by the organization that portray an image of dependency and vulnerability for the purpose of soliciting assistance from others.	Domestic firms that emphasize their vulnerability to foreign competition while lobbying for tariffs and other forms of trade protection.

Note. Adapted from "A Taxonomy of Organizational Impression Management Tactics,"by A. Mohamed, W. Gardner, and J. Paolillo, 1999, Advances in Competitiveness Research, 7(1), p. 5. Reprinted with permission.

Table 3 Direct/Defensive Organizational Impression Management Tactics

Behavior	Definition/Description	Example
Accounts	Explanations of a predicament-creating event that seek to minimize the apparent severity of the predicament.	Top management downplays the severity of their firm's bankruptcy, stating that Chapter 11 really means" there's still hope."
Disclaimers	Explanations given prior to a potentially embarrassing action to ward off any negative repercussions for the actor's image.	Notices by brokerage firms that warn performance is not guaranteed for the future.
Organizational handicapping	Efforts by an organization to make task success appear unlikely to provide a ready-made excuse for failure.	Remarks by an aerospace manufacturer's CEO that it is unlikely to outbid a French firm for a foreign contract

because it is subsidized by the French government.

Apologies	Admissions of blameworthiness for a negative event, which include expressions of remorse and requests for a pardon.	A manager tells a customer, "We're sorry for the delay in shipping your order. We pride ourselves on timely deliveries, but we slipped up this time. Please forgive us."
Restitution	Offers of compensation that are extended by the organization to the offended, injured, or otherwise harmed audience.	Airline passengers who are bumped from a flight due to overbooking are provided with vouchers for free round-trip tickets to any domestic

	destination of their choice.	
Pro-social behavior	Engaging in pro-social actions to atone for an apparent transgression and convince an audience that the actor merits a positive identity.	A southern university attempts to atone for past racial discrimination by offering an extensive array of minority scholarships and aggressively hiring minority faculty and administrators.

Note. Adapted from "A Taxonomy of Organizational Impression Management Tactics," by A. Mohamed, W. Gardner, and J. Paolillo, 1999, *Advances in Competitiveness Research,* 7(1), p. 5. Reprinted with permission.

Table 4 Indirect Organizational Impression Management Tactics

Behavior	Definition/Description	Example
	Assertive Tactics	
	Connection-Focused Tactics	
Boasting	Proclaiming a positive link to a favorable other.	An advertising campaign that portrays a firm as an "official" sponsor of the U.S. Olympic team.
Blaring	Proclaiming a negative link to an unfavorable other.	7-Up ads that inform customers that the "UnCola" is caffeine-free ("Never had it, Never will")
	Other-Focused Tactics	
Burnishing	Enhancing the favorable features of a positively linked other.	A business that extols the virtues of a local sports team.
Blasting	Exaggerating the unfavorable features of a negatively linked other.	FedEx advertisements that humorously portray rival express mail delivery firms as slow, unreliable, and grossly inept.

Defensive Tactics		
Connection Focused Tactics		
Burying	Disclaiming or obscuring a positive link to an unfavorable other.	Saturn Corporation's decision not to display GM's logo on its automobiles or literature.
Blurring	Disclaiming or obscuring a negative link to a favorable other.	A university's administration downplays its past opposition to a popular faculty union.

Defensive Tactics		
Connection Focused Tactics		
Burying	Disclaiming or obscuring a positive link to an unfavorable other.	Saturn Corporation's decision not to display GM's logo on its automobiles or literature.
Blurring	Disclaiming or obscuring a negative link to a favorable other.	A university's administration downplays its past opposition to a popular faculty union.

Boosting	Minimizing the unfavorable features of a positively linked other.	A corporation that downplays the sexual and violent content of a TV show it sponsors.
Belittling	Minimizing the favorable traits of a negatively linked other.	An economy hotel chain that describes the luxurious accommodation of an upscale rival as unnecessary frills that produce inflated room rates.

Note. Adapted from "A Taxonomy of Organizational Impression Management Tactics," by A. Mohamed, W. Gardner, and J. Paolillo, 1999, Advances in Competitiveness Research, 7(1), p. 9. Reprinted with permission.

In summary, while research has focused on the effects of individual IM in the workplace, few studies have been done on organization's use of IM strategy (Bolino et al., 2008). Those that have studied OIM have used the taxonomy developed by Mohamed et al. (2008) to some degree. The following section outlines studies that have shown OIM used as a strategic tool by companies in their advertising campaigns. Organizational impression management has been used in corporate social responsibility campaigns, cause-related marketing, damage control, and creation of desired brand or organizational image. These actions are all related to enhancing, maintaining, and creating organizational image as part of OIM strategy (Matejek & Gössling, 2014). They can further be identified with the categories on the OIM taxonomy (Mohamed et al., 1999). Assertive tactics on the OIM taxonomy include corporate social responsibility (CSR) campaigns, cause-related marketing (CRM), and other communications boasting successes of the organization. Damage control, a defensive tactic on the OIM taxonomy, includes negating or avoiding damaging publicity. Through careful communications with all stakeholders, organizations are able to control their public image. Following are examples of how OIM has been studied in marketing campaigns and other communications through CSR, CRM, brand management, reputation enhancement, and damage control.

Corporate social responsibility (CSR). Part of marketing strategy is to enhance an organization's image or reputation and to show a commitment for improving the community at large. Corporate social responsibility consists of company involvement with charitable causes or the nonprofit organizations that represent them (Chang, 2008). Corporate social responsibility behaviors are voluntary activities by a corporation to enhance community well-being through discretionary business practices or resource contributions, of which the benefits can be economic, social, or environmental.

Organizations try to enhance their reputations by engaging in certain business practices, announcing their involvement with social issues, and making monetary or corporate resource contributions to worthy causes. Thus, they can be viewed as being socially responsible. In this manner, CSR is a form of assertive OIM behavior in which the organization seeks to enhance its reputation. CSR is a form of exemplification (Highhouse et al., 2009). It exemplifies the company boasting of its commitment to furthering social causes. As such, it can be classified as a direct assertive behavior. If used as an anticipatory tactic, for example, in anticipation of bad publicity, it can be classified on the OIM taxonomy as a form a direct defensive prosocial behavior (Tyler et al., 2012).

Corporate reputation can be defined as the overall organizational impression as reflected through perceptions of collective stakeholders (Lai, Chiu, Yang, & Pai, 2010). The company web site has become the primary communication vehicle for organizations to manage their identities and present their desired image to stakeholders. Conveyance of this identity is crucial in positioning efforts. A study of financial institution's company web sites revealed that publicly posting CSR activities can be a critical factor in targeting and influencing stakeholders. Certain organizations were more likely to incorporate their CSR activities not only on their web site communications but also within their corporate cultures and statements (Bravo et al., 2012).

Another study looked at the differences of consumer's impressions between marketer-created social networking sites and consumer-related sites. The focus of the study was to determine whether consumers felt that the corporation's purpose was profit- motivated or altruistic. The sample consisted of 120 college students who participated in fictional online brand communities, either marketer-created or consumer-created. The community participants indicated how they felt regarding their own social identification and motivation for joining and then rated the company's motives for hosting the site. The outcome was that consumer-related social networking sites were seen as more authentic and more altruistic than the company sites (Doohwang et al., 2011). Limitations of the study were that intentions, but not actual purchasing behaviors, were documented and that the product used was fictional. However, the sense of an organization hosting consumer-based forums was a form of OIM in maintaining that the company was transparent and, therefore honest, in its motives. Claims of honesty, present concern, and virtue are related to reputational management strategies (Craig & Brennan, 2012).

A different study on CSR campaigns took into account customer viewpoints of campaign effectiveness on overall impression of brand equity. Based on 179 questionnaires that Lai et al. (2010) sent to manufacturing companies, CSR campaigns had a positive effect on organizational reputation and brand performance. Although done in a small market sector of industrial buyers, the study also found that brand equity increased with an increase in CSR campaigns. As with prior studies, publicly announcing CSR activities was regarded as a strategic OIM move to enhance consumer perceptions of company image (Lai et al., 2010).

CSR activities can be regarded as using direct assertive tactics of organizational promotion and exemplification (McDonnell & King, 2013). In particular, the OIM direct assertive tactic of exemplification is often used when a company wants to portray a favorable image through acts of CSR (Avery & McKay, 2006). Avery and McKay (2006) used Mohamed et al.'s (1999) OIM taxonomy to study IM in recruiting minorities and females. The framework of the study measured only the direct categories of the taxonomy: direct/assertive and direct/defensive behaviors. The researchers found that some organizational image efforts are indeed the motive behind CSR campaigns. Examples were using CSR efforts to sponsor events and various organizations connected with women and minorities (Avery & McKay, 2006). Thus, the company was perceived as being socially responsible and embracing diversity.

As in the previous example, CSR activities are considered an OIM strategy for rebounding from negative publicity. A recent article discussed the issue of reputational legitimacy and the process of repairing image as OIM tactics. *Legitimacy* was defined as a perception that the actions of the organization are proper and appropriate within socially constructed norms, values, and beliefs (Matejek & Gössling, 2014). This concept correlates with IM theory of maintaining organizational image. Matejek and Gössling (2014) studied BP, Inc., after the catastrophe surrounding the Gulf of Mexico environmental disaster. The researchers studied BP's "green image" campaign after BP was accused of corporate fraud and misleading statements. They explored BP's green initiative in light of accusations that it was a form of deception and claims that it was actual material change in organizational goals. The units of analysis were narrative texts following the catastrophe, including press releases, web site postings, ads, and corporate sustainability reports. The finding was that BP's OIM initiatives profited from the campaign initially, yet stakeholders came to doubt the motives behind the green campaign and felt misled by the company. Thus, its legitimacy and reputational image were questioned, whereby BP eventually became more cautious in responding to negative publicity. The lesson from this case was to ensure the authenticity of symbolic actions on which IM is based. Limitations were that the study focused on the OIM effects rather than the deliberate or intentional strategies of the company. Stakeholders viewed BP's "greening campaign" as a self-serving means in fulfilling organizational agendas and regulatory compliance. Its OIM campaign eventually reversed these effects, and OIM strategies were successful in building legitimacy (Matejek & Gössling, 2014).

In conclusion, CSR can be used as a competitive advantage. Research has shown that most organizations voluntarily disclose their CSR activities in order to legitimize their behaviors and construct their identities (Bravo et al., 2012). Press releases are another mode of communication to relay CSR activities to various audiences. According to Brennan et al. (2013), CSR is a function of the power relationship between organizations and stakeholders. It can take the form of crisis communication since organizational responsiveness is critical in maintaining favorable image (Brennan et al.,2013). Therefore, conveying a socially responsible image and maintaining favorable stakeholder relations have become important marketing goals for organizations.

Cause-related marketing (CRM). Yet another part of marketing strategy is making the consumer part of the cause, whether through purchase or behavior. A derivative of CSR is cause-related marketing campaigns (CRM), which tie the philanthropic donation to a purchase to achieve organizational goals (Chang, 2008). Examples include asking consumers to contribute money to a cause each time they make a purchase or telling the consumer that the company will donate to a cause upon purchase. The organization thus enhances its image as an active social participant by inviting consumers to become actively involved with a cause. In this capacity, the company is acting in an ingratiating manner, a direct assertive OIM tactic (Mohamed et al., 1999).

As explained above, CRM campaigns often entice consumers to act in a certain way, either through making donations or changing behaviors. Jin and Lee (2010) wanted to see if real-world behaviors transferred to a social networking virtual world, and vice- versa, to examine brand satisfaction and trust. At the crux of their model was whether consumers experienced "regulatory fit" with the brand. *Regulatory fit* refers to how well consumers see the brand fit with their self-concept. Jin and Lee's sample consisted of

103 college students who were assigned in either regulatory fit or misfit conditions. The students participated in a 3-D script in the virtual world entitled *Second Life,* involving a health avatar that dispensed health information. The purpose of the study was to see if real-world health behaviors were altered after consumers consulted with a health avatar. Findings showed that these consumers initially experienced greater brand satisfaction and trust than those who did not, and developed healthier habits in real life. Although the study did not record consumer's actual purchasing behaviors, it provided a solid basis for use of CRM in organizational marketing pursuits (Jin & Lee, 2010).

Cause-related marketing can also mean that the organization makes some sort of contribution based on sales, revenues, or other consumer-driven factor. Often, CRM and CSR overlap in this respect. Michelon (2011) studied organization's social responsibility disclosures on financial, social, and environmental information. The purpose of the study was to see whether internal or financial motivation was the driver for disclosure. Prior research had not revealed a clear relationship between financial performance and CSR disclosures, so Michelon set out to see whether disclosure was more attributed to CRM.

Commitment and engagement with stakeholders, along with increased media exposure, were the elements positively associated with higher sustainability disclosure. Furthermore, the study suggested that sustainability disclosure was an intentionally strategic act driven by preservation of public reputation (Michelon, 2011). This is a direct assertive behavior of organizational promotion (Mohamed et al., 1999).

More recently, researchers have considered the effect of online media platforms and CRM. One study looked at self-image from a consumer's viewpoint, concluding that organizations should consider the type of social media platform when trying to engage consumers through OIM tactics (Hyun Ju & Mira, 2013). Social behavior is often a product of how individuals and organizations portray themselves to others, yet this study showed the choice of media platform had a profound effect. Hyun Ju and Mira (2013) found that consumers preferred interactive social networking sites over non-interactive online sites. Social media sites that were interactive and visible to others were found to increase interest and membership among consumers (Hyun Ju & Mira, 2013). In other words, consumers preferred a platform in which they could also demonstrate a form of IM to others. The ability of the platform to showcase both consumer and organizational commitment to causes, therefore, is an important factor to consider in CRM campaigns. Philanthropy and claims of social responsibility represent the OIM category of exemplification (Pollach & Kerbler, 2011).

In conclusion, messages sent by organizations can produce favorable attitudes, enrich advocacy behaviors among stakeholders, and generate stronger corporate image. The message can be related to specific social causes or can draw attention to the organization's commitment to the cause. Most focus on the latter, with messages of company contributions, donations, or provision of other resources directly to the cause. It is important that the organization itself has a perceived fit with the cause (Du et al.,2010). Both CSR- and CRM-related communications are tied to organizational image and can build corporate identity and foster better stakeholder relations. According to Du et al. (2010), it is important to convey these messages yet not appear to have intrinsic motives in these marketing efforts.

Brand image and damage control. Perhaps the most popular reason for engaging in OIM is to fulfill the mission of an organization's marketing strategy. This can be accomplished by enhancing company image and soliciting favorable brand recognition, while warding off negative publicity. Examples of organizational assertive and defensive tactics were identified by Mohamed et al. (1999). The assertive tactics were identified as ingratiation, intimidation, organizational promotion, exemplification, and supplication (Mohamed et al., 1999). The six defensive tactics to restore or protect organizational image are accounts, disclaimers, organizational handicapping, apologies, restitution, and pro-social behavior (Avery & McKay, 2006). Tactics can further be defined within each category. For example, the defensive category of accounts can be classified as denials, apologies, justifications, or excuses. Avery and McKay (2006) found that organizations under fire for discrimination commonly use denial as a defensive tactic.

As such, the themes discussed are related to marketing efforts to enhance, maintain, and control company image. In this sense, OIM tactics can help an organization appeal to stakeholders with well-targeted messages that portray the image it intends to project. Organizational impression management tactics have been studied across a variety of platforms, including analysis of initial public offerings, press releases, company financial graphs, and other communications vehicles. Some of these studies are highlighted below. It is essential to note the different communications vehicles observed in OIM research in order to later contrast social media as a platform. The following represent OIM research on traditional platforms, while relatively few studies have been done on OIM via social media. It is important to understand what has been accomplished in prior studies in order to fully appreciate the medium of social media.

Initial public offerings. Brand image IM has often been used in initial public offerings of a firm's stock and to manage perceptions of new venture legitimacy (Lamertz & Martens, 2011; Nagy et al., 2012). The initial public offering (IPO) document aims to convince investors of the firm's potential as a public enterprise. A major part of an IPO is persuasion of the organization's worth, and another part is making sure that those associated with an organization are comfortable enough to endorse an IPO. An organization that issues an IPO is regulated by the Securities and Exchange Commission (SEC) and is held to disclosure of all known risks the company may face that could cause loss of value (Lamertz & Martens, 2011).

Using the IPO as the vehicle for OIM, Lamertz and Martens (2011) conducted an IM study to see how institutional factors influence and persuade potential investors. The sample was of 167 U.S. organizations from three different industries that issued IPOs between 1996 and 2000. The data were collected entirely from the IPO prospectus. Data were either placed into a Risk Factor category, whereupon organizations disclosed negative elements, or in Strategy Sections and Governance Provisions categories, which focused upon the positive IPO aspects. The results showed that organizations minimized poor qualities and maximized their best qualities when attempting an IPO. Further, dependence on other professional firms and the endorsement of an IPO network assisted in shaping the desired images before an IPO.

Financial graphs. In some instances, companies have manipulated financial graphs to alter the presentation of information. Huang et al. (2011) researched the effects of OIM of financial graphs presented on company websites. The items studied were presentation materials for stakeholders and investors, including audited and unaudited items. They concluded that stock price pressures influence companies to adjust financial graphs improperly. Although they studied several countries, including Taiwan and China, they found that organizations in the U.S. tended to show more financial graphs when performance was better, to emphasize positive performance, than when it was not. Hence, the researchers concluded that organizations use OIM for self-interest and to manipulate their image to stakeholders (Huang et al., 2011).

Annual reports. However, Zeller et al. (2012) found that few Standard & Poor's (S&P) 500 companies used IM tactics on their annual reports. The 7-year longitudinal study concluded that companies included complete sets of financial and nonfinancial information on the annual report to shareholders per SEC requirements. However, companies selectively disclosed voluntary information to shareholders, if any at all (Zeller et al., 2012). Disclosure credibility can also be measured not only by what companies say but also by how they state the information. Negative information was at times manipulated by the intentional complexity of writing or even by blaming circumstances outside the organization's control. Repetition and over-emphasis of positive information was used in the same way (Rahman, 2012).

Prospectuses. In another study, Halim and Jaafar (2012) questioned whether organizational strategy of voluntary information disclosure had significant potential for changing investor's perceptions of an organization. They researched the top 200 Australian companie's annual reports and prospectuses to measure the extent of disclosure. Other voluntary intangibles analyzed included company highlights, chairman's statements, CEO reviews, community involvement, and social responsibility statements. Halim and Jaafar found that the level of disclosure in regulated documents, such as prospectuses, was lower than annual reports because of stringent reporting requirements. Annual reports that were not as regularly audited or regulated had more intangible information available. Halim and Jaafar speculated that organizations limited the amount of disclosure in prospectuses to actively control information and prevent disclosure of misleading information.

Bills and invoices. Accordingly, research on damage control has focused on providing remedies to negative situations and diffusing the fallout. Researchers Tyler et al. (2012) set out to find if anticipatory OIM tactics prevented negative situations or challenges from occurring in the first place. Anticipatory tactics were aimed at prevention of negative situations or negative images. Language and specific verbiage used in hospital billing was manipulated to see if it reduced the number of customers questioning the bill and prevented negative company image. Indeed, the research findings suggested that anticipatory tactics in situations where challenge is likely effectively diffused negative reactions (Tyler et al., 2012). This portion of the study corresponded to the OIM tactics of legitimacy and accommodation.

Yet another experiment by the same researchers used anticipatory OIM tactics to create an image of organizational bureaucracy. Findings showed that when presented with images of bureaucracy, most customers felt helpless to change course and challenge their bill (Tyler et al., 2012). These tactics corresponded to the OIM tactics of intimidation and fear. Thus, in both experiments, the OIM tactics worked as intended.

Reputation management. Impression management plays a role in overall organizational reputation (Mohamed et al., 2008; O'Keefe & Conway, 2008; Pollach & Kerbler, 2011; Vielhaber & Waltman, 2008; Westphal, Park, McDonald, & Hayward, 2012). Accounting literature has revealed that, especially when faced with challenges, organizations can effectively manage threats that can affect their reputation (O'Keefe & Conway, 2008). Optimism in letters to shareholders, responses to negative publicity, and CEO profiles have been studied to see if they affect reputational image management and damage control.

The popularity of corporate rankings has a much do with the interest in reputations (Highhouse et al., 2009). In a review of the research on corporate reputations, Highhouse et al. (2009) concluded that CSR activities and other communications have made the corporation a social actor, much as individuals practice IM. The reputation of an organization is, thus, a collective perception by others. The corporation desires approval, aspires for status, and is concerned with image and presentation. Cues that organizations can directly manipulate are advertising, public relations, and CSR policies. Highhouse et al. divided these activities into symbolic and substantive actions, whereby symbolic actions are comprised of advertising, public relations, and CSR. Substantive activities include social, human, or product development capital investments and diversification. All of these cues are involved in proactively endorsing the organizational image.

CEO letters to shareholders. Patelli and Pedrini (2013) studied the usage and effect of optimism in CEO letters to shareholders to see if there was an association with firm performance. Specifically, they looked at the rhetorical tone of over 300 CEO letters to shareholders from a sampling of *Fortune 500* companies in 15 industries during the economic crisis of 2008-2009. Patelli and Pedrini used the software Diction to examine the association of optimistic tone and financial performance. Diction has been used to assess *Certainty* and *Optimism* in different types of communications mechanisms, from political speeches to all types of corporate documents. The *Certainty* and *Optimism* dictionaries have been associated with the Direct Assertive category on the Mohamed et al. (1999) taxonomy of OIM in several recent studies (Brennan et al., 2008; Craig & Brennan, 2012; Hall et al., 2013; Patelli & Pedrini, 2013). Optimistic tone emphasizes positive news, while de-emphasizing negative publicity. Patelli and Pedrini concluded that optimism was positively correlated with better future financial performance, suggesting that the positive tone in CEO letters was an indication of firm financial performance. Nonetheless, they suggested that the sincerity of CEO letters was legitimate, and those with better financial performance were, therefore, more optimistic in tone.

Other studies have shown that firms do engage in IM through CEO letters to shareholders. CEO letters are important communication channels because they are not mandatory, and most large companies voluntarily disclose information they feel is important (Patelli & Pedrini, 2013). Organizations have been suspected of engaging in IM based on the assumption that they exaggerate successes and underplay failures (Merkl-Davies & Brennan, 2007). However, Patelli and Pedrini (2013) did not find this to be true. They did find an association between engaging verbiage in CEO letters to shareholders and overall financial performance, but that disclosure was sincere in the firms they studied.

Craig and Brennan (2012) looked at the association of CEO letters and corporate reputation. They identified the top 100 U.S. companies ranked in *Fortune 500 Magazine* for annual earnings and recorded them based on whether they held high or low reputation, which was considered distinct from corporate image. *Reputation* was defined as the actual attributes that others use to describe a company, whereas *corporate image* was how the company believed others described them. Craig and Brennan analyzed the CEO letters to shareholders in terms of language selection for the purposes of IM. Their findings suggested there was not a statistically significant relationship between language choice of CEO letters and corporate reputation (Craig & Brennan, 2012). However, they concluded that more research could establish an association, and perhaps demographically different stakeholders may view company reputation differently.

Rahman (2012) also suggested that IM strategies may not work, especially in context of the current global credit crisis. In contrast, Merkl-Davies and Brennan (2007) found that CEO letters were a perfect vehicle for IM and that obfuscation of financial information was achieved through either non-disclosure or manipulation of data through visual, effects, tone, and choice of company performance metrics.

News stories. Likewise, Tetlock et al. (2008) argued that unexpected negative publicity can trigger defensive IM strategies. Through content analysis using the Harvard IV psychosocial dictionary, they researched verbiage in news stories of S&P 500 firms to predict firm's earnings and returns. Their assumption was that negative language in the *Wall Street Journal* and Dow Jones Service would negatively impact company stock returns. In particular, they did a content analysis of the fraction of negative words appearing in over 350,000 news articles. Their findings were that negative stories contribute to measuring a company's fundamentals; therefore, linguistic measures were just as valid as quantitative measures in forecasting earnings (Tetlock et al., 2008).

Thus, a problem for organizations is how to effectively manage negative publicity in an era where the public has control. Kucuk (2010) stated that it is nearly impossible to do an Internet search for a highly recognized brand name and not come across some negative publicity. The purpose of Kucuk's study was to determine how much damage and for how long negative publicity can hurt an organization. A leading search engine was used to find anti-brand sites by searching with negative terms associated with company names. The findings were that anti-brand websites of the top 100 global brands had increased in triplicate between the years 2005 and 2009. Most of the anti-brand web sites did not survive more than four years, but the negative publicity was still disseminated.

Accordingly, IM can be used to diffuse negative publicity based on CEO reputation. In a study by Westphal et al. (2012), 367 CEOs of public companies with over $100 million in sales were polled to determine the effects of IM in communications between CEOs and journalists. The CEOs responded to questionnaires between 1999 and 2007. The researchers found that a firm's reputation with stakeholders and the public is influenced by journalist's reports based on the impressions of CEOs following reports of negative earnings.

CEO profiles. The impact of CEO profiles and personal reputation on the organization has been studied in other research under the framework of IM (Nagy et al.,2012). Pollach and Kerbler (2011) used content analysis to assess the assertive IM tactics in U.S. CEO profiles presented on corporate web sites as compared to those of European CEO profiles. In their sample of top companies on the *Fortune Global 500* list, they found that the reputation of the CEO has profound effect on an organization's effectiveness, reputation, and financial stock recommendations. *CEO competence* was defined as the bundle of knowledge, skills, and behaviors portrayed on corporate web sites. Pollach and Kerbler looked at the CEO's social political, and public life. Press nominations and political activities of CEOs were more prominently displayed in the U.S. corporation's websites.Nagy et al. (2012) assessed that entrepreneur's IM behaviors could influence stakeholder's perceptions of new venture legitimacy. *Legitimacy* was defined as acceptance, appropriateness, and worthiness made about entrepreneurs and the efforts they portray through credentials and other narratives. The researchers studied the IM tactics of ingratiation, self-promotion, and exemplification to determine if these tactics had an effect on the perceptions formed by stakeholders. They found that entrepreneurs can affect the perceptions of new venture legitimacy through targeted IM behaviors (Nagy et al., 2012).

O'Keefe and Conway (2008) searched news websites to identify negative publicity that potentially affected the content of non-governmental organization's CEO letters prior to a natural disaster. The researchers used content analysis to code CEO letters according to Mohamed et al.'s (1999) OIM taxonomy of direct behaviors. They found that there was no significant increase in direct assertive or direct defensive IM tactics after a natural disaster, and surprisingly, the number of defensive tactics actually decreased. Their findings were inconsistent with IM theory, which claims that defensive strategies and assertive tactics should increase in response to threats (O'Keefe & Conway, 2008).

Technology has allowed many communication options as an advantage but, at the same time, have proven troublesome for organizations in crisis situations. Because of instantaneous response and widespread readership, technology can provide consistent and credible messages to protect company image yet can also facilitate the travel of bad publicity (Vielhaber & Waltman, 2008). The anti-branding sites explored by Kucuk (2010) showed just how prevalent negative publicity can be on social networking sites.

An illustration of the effects of negative publicity was shown by Muthukrishnan and Chattopadhyay (2007), who maintained that a bad first impression is the sign of a significant brand image problem. The purpose of their study was to test if consumers tend to remember the specifics of bad publicity more than they remember good publicity. The research consisted of four experiments, with 194 participants in the first experiment. The first experiment divided the group into those who had received positive product information and those who had received negative information; then, participants were given conflicting information. At the end, they had to evaluate the product. The second, third, and fourth experiments were quite similar in nature, other than manipulation of variables and stimulants. In all experiments, the product used was a pen, which is not a major consumer purchase. One of the major findings was that comparative challenges are more effective in changing positive image, and non-comparative challenges are more effective in changing negative images. Major limitations of this study were that the brand was fictitious and was not considered a consequential purchase compared to other products.

Crisis communication is also a form of damage control (Vielhaber & Waltman,

2008). It has become an important part of corporate reporting with the purpose of enhancing organizational reputation and maintaining credibility. Vielhaber and Waltman (2008) studied targeted communications on web sites and other electronic measures, such as press releases, blogs, emails, and web site postings. Through examination of their own responses, organizations can see if their messages are defensive or accommodative and observe which communication channels can help provide consistent and clear information to stakeholders.

Business plans. The content analysis of linguistic elements in business plans was the topic of focus in another OIM study using Diction 7.0 software. Parhankangas and Ehrlich (2012) studied the verbal tone of business plans and the chances of raising money through angel funding. Angel investments are nontraditional sources of external funding for new ventures (Parhankangas & Ehrlich, 2012). The analysis found that those who received funding engaged in indirect IM behaviors. These indirect behaviors, such as self-criticism, and promotion of competition had a mitigating effect on the negativity of blasting the competition. Outright direct OIM behaviors of blasting the competition had a negative effect on organizations, thereby decreasing their chances of angel funding (Parhankangas & Ehrlich, 2012). The researchers contend that analysis of verbal tone beyond content was key to their study on how organizations achieve desired outcomes.

Press releases. Press releases have also been scrutinized for OM tactics due to their public access on company web sites. Studies of press releases and annual reports, both financial and non-financial, reveal IM is pervasive in corporate narratives. Press releases are often voluntary and unregulated, which makes them a perfect vehicle for IM. A study of bias in corporate narratives showed that positive information was often exaggerated, and negative facts and statistics were understated (Brennan et al., 2008). Brennan et al. (2008) used 101 press releases and a list of 301 keywords from prior OIM research to identify OIM tactics in corporate annual press releases. A resulting composite OIM measure was based on IM techniques that were used in following studies.

Osma and Guillamón-Saorín (2009) used the Brennan et al. (2008) measure to study the relationship between corporate governance and OIM behaviors. *Corporate governance* was identified as either corporate or non-corporate boards that regulated and monitored the actions of mangers in the interest of investors and other stakeholders. Organizational impression management tactics were identified through annual corporate results posted in press releases. The mixed-methods study showed that qualitative information was used when the company had negative news to disclose, and quantitative information was released when positive information was disclosed. The resulting finding was that strong corporate governance limits the amount of OIM used by companies. Managers in weak governance companies presented information in ways that both limited and distorted company information in order to influence reader's perceptions (Osma & Guillamón-Saorín, 2009).

Accordingly, in a study of damage control and reputation, Chilcutt (2009) conducted a content analysis of the United State's most profitable low fare, high frequency airline. Chilcutt studied 18 episodes of the reality television show *Airline*, which featured Southwest Airlines and filmed how the airlines dealt with problems. The purpose of the study was to examine the relevance and effectiveness of Mohamed et al.'s 1999 taxonomy. Chilcutt found that even in negative situations, organizations have the ability to create positive perceptions. The study further validated the OIM taxonomy and its usefulness for dealing with organizational stakeholders. As illustrated above, OIM communications vehicles encompass any and all communications that organizations choose to share with their stakeholders. Information can be controlled on platforms ranging from press releases to CEO profiles. The motivation behind OIM is to protect company image, brand, and reputation, while combatting negative reviews. Concluding this discussion is an examination of the role social media plays in organizational communications. In terms of OIM, social media is a platform that can have greater consequences than traditional forms of communications due to rapid exposure and wider accessibility (Hale, 2010).

OIM via social media. Thus far, OIM has been studied through press releases, CEO letters to shareholders, annual reports, financial graphs, news stories, IPOs, and reality television shows. Social media has become an important outlet to consider in the study of OIM, mainly because technology has changed traditional communications with stakeholders (Boyd & Ellison, 2007; Rahman, 2012; Vielhaber & Waltman, 2008). *Social media sites* can be defined as internet-based services that allow users to construct a profile within a circumscribed system, whether public or semi-private; share some sort of connection with other users; and view and have access to connections and those made by others within the system (Boyd & Ellison, 2007).

An early study on OIM was conducted by Winter et al. (2003), who wanted to learn whether consumers were influenced by organizational web sites. Indeed, web sites influenced potential consumer's impressions of organizational legitimacy and image. The researchers found that web site visitors form impression of symbols, graphics, and other content on organizational web pages. An implication of these early findings was that businesses should recognize and explore further the power of IM of web sites. The sample was of university students who were not actual customers, but nonetheless, their research opened the door to the study of websites, with all their symbolic content, and organizational image control. Winter et al. found that websites can influence perceptions of an organization and implored further research into generalizing findings to other populations and industries (Winter et al., 2003).

Thus, organizational websites still remain the most common tool for communicating the "public face" of an organization and serve as the main portal to an organization's social media (Saxton & Guo, 2012). The content of a website reflects the way organizations wish to be perceived. Saxton and Guo (2012) examined the relationship between website stakeholder communications and consequent level of charitable donations. They conducted a two-part inductive analysis to identify communication practices through websites and found that organizations can effectively use them as a tool for targeting stakeholders and managing impressions (Saxton & Guo,2012). In addition, most organizational websites are often the gateway to any other social media.

Social media and social networking fall under Web 2.0 activities, which have changed the relationship between businesses and consumers by allowing community- building and consumer-generated content. Social media has the capability to rapidly transmit mass communications between consumers, businesses, and a combination of both, which separates it from traditional media (Hale, 2010). Social media sites have also been referred to as *computer-mediated communications* (CMC), the process of using technology as an information exchange platform. Although CMCs have been around for a few decades, the most notable are Facebook, LinkedIn, YouTube, and Twitter. Self- presentation and organizational image can be controlled on social media sites, since their interactive nature allows users to actively manage their profiles. This control is more apparent in social media than in traditional forms of communications (Boyd & Ellison,2007). Because of this control, organizations can strategically manage what is included or censored and, therefore, actively manage their public impressions. Where once media professionals and other communication staffs were used to circulate company information, organizations now have the instantaneous ability to alter and control information dissemination. Technology expands communication options, especially in a crisis; facilitates instant communication; and can provide consistent and credible messages to protect organizational image (Vielhaber & Waltman, 2008).

Before social media, OIM research focused on extracting tactics from mass media, annual reports, or other traditional communication vehicles. Social media has facilitated information sharing and interactive, collaborative web platforms that have been useful in IM strategies (Schniederjans et al., 2013). Boyd and Ellison (2007) studied the relationship between Facebook and *social capital*, defined as the resources accumulated through relationships. They found that a strong association existed between use of social media and social capital, including self-esteem and presentation of image (Boyd & Ellison, 2007).

Facebook has been the most popular social media site to study, especially for individual IM behaviors. Facebook began in 2004 and has expanded to over 120 million global users. It currently is the largest social network and has 845 million active users. Impression management formation is a central element for users and an attestation to the popularity of Facebook (Hall et al., 2013). Recent studies looked at IM on Facebook from an individual perspective. Some organizations have a Facebook page for communications, but mostly, it is used for personal communications of a single user.

Facebook has increasingly become the vehicle for most organizations to communicate with consumers. Kwok and Yu (2013) examined the types of social media messages used by hospitality companies and their effect on Facebook users. Through Facebook queries, they compared the messages sent by the top restaurants and hotels and the "likes" initiated by consumers. The tone of the message had an effect, with marketing-related messages being less popular than informational messages (Kwok & Yu, 2013). Company Facebook pages with photos, graphics, and updates on company status were also more popular than those without them. Informational messages appear to be more popular than traditional sales-related messages among younger consumers; thus, marketing communications have been forever transformed. Although Facebook remains popular among younger users, law firms have been slow to adopt social media in general and Facebook in particular (Fairley, 2013), a phenomenon that will be discussed in the final section of this literature review.

Likewise, Twitter started in 2006 and has grown exponentially to over 50 million global users (Hambrick, Simmons, Greenhalgh, & Greenwell, 2010). Twitter users can follow other users and post messages, called "tweets," of up to 140 characters on their own Twitter accounts. These tweets are short messages and publicly available, making them convenient to research. Often used to connect to a fan base, Twitter has become a popular vehicle for professional communications and is used by established media sources (Lovejoy et al., 2012). The 140-character limit effectively makes it a micro-blogging application and ideal for marketing and public relations to stakeholders. According to one source, Twitter is the largest micro-blogging site on the internet and is used by businesses to promote their products and services as well as solicit consumer feedback (Lovejoy et al., 2012). Twitter has a decidedly older audience, since estimates place just 11% of its users under the age of 17 (Hambrick et al., 2010; Lovejoy et al.,2012; Miller, 2009). Through identification of business communications via online social networks, researchers can assess how they are used to effectively communicate their messages (Hambrick et al., 2010). Previous studies have examined Twitter for marketing,

identity management, trend monitoring, brand management, and data mining (Mathioudakis & Koudas, 2010). Because of its popularity, the present study used Twitter to examine social media communications of law firms.

Another recent study looked at organization's creative ways to utilize the 140 character limit per tweet. Lovejoy et al. (2012) conducted a computer-aided content analysis of tweets of the largest revenue-grossing U.S. firms listed in the *Nonprofit Times 100*. Out of 100 firms, 73 had Twitter accounts. Lovejoy et al. found that large nonprofit firms are not using Twitter to engage stakeholders but, rather, used Twitter as a one-way communication tool. Twitter messages can reach a large number of stakeholders very quickly, and for this reason, Twitter has become the most-used social media for public relations and marketing (Lovejoy et al., 2012). An important finding is that organizations are not using Twitter for interpersonal communications but for managing stakeholder impressions.

Social networking has been defined as the new marketing channel. Organizations can use these sites as strategic channels to gain larger audience exposure, attract new prospects, tap into related networks, establish connections with other businesses, and establish controlled impressions (Hale, 2010). They can leverage influence over their social network audience and created company credibility by becoming what Hale (2010) calls "content creators and publishers" (p. 5).

The same marketing activities defined earlier appear on organizational social media pages. For example, CRM campaigns can be easily adapted to social media, and the organization can create interactivity, such as giving consumers an opportunity to donate an extra dollar to a cause by clicking a link (Chang, 2008). CRM campaigns are often found on brand pages as donations to Special Olympics or as contributions for cancer research. In addition to organizational benefits, consumers promote their own IM by being seen as someone who is a cause supporter on a public platform (Leary & Kowalski, 1990). From the prior discussion on CRM campaigns, the types of social media platforms affected consumer's willingness and intent to join a cause (Hyun & Mira, 2013). Hyun and Mira (2013) found that social networking sites were more effective than internet sites classified as non-social networking sites. In other words, the visibility of the social media platform had a role in the intentions to join a cause. Hyun and Mira posited that social media has become an important tool for organizations to develop strategies.

The growth of social media provides opportunity yet is a cause of concern for organizations trying to manage image control. Schniederjans et al. (2013) set out to determine whether direct assertive strategies in social media have an effect on a company's financial performance. They used text mining on forums, blogs, and organizational websites and analyzed it based on financial performance of the organizations studied. The study used the direct assertive strategies taken from the Mohamed et al. (1999) taxonomy. Schniederjans et al.'s findings showed a positive relationship between the use of assertive OIM tactics and financial rankings. Consequently, organizations use OIM to influence the way stakeholders view the organization and for other various marketing-related reasons (Bolino et al., 2008). However, consumers now hold the balance of power due to social media, and organizations should embrace the opportunity to converse, understand, and find ways to transform the negative complaints into positive experiences (Kucuk, 2010).

Organizations must respond quickly to negative publicity and anti-branding to reverse the situation.

To summarize, OIM has not been studied as extensively as IM, and studies of OIM within social media are fairly recent (Avery & McKay, 2006; Bolino et al., 2008; Schniederjans et al., 2013). The studies conducted by Doohwang et al. (2011), Jin and Lee (2010), Lamertz and Martens (2011), and Kucuk (2010) all indicate a need for careful image management in social media. Whether the purpose is marketing or damage control, competitive organizations must be cognizant of their projected public image and have defense mechanisms in place to combat negative publicity and anti-branding on social media sites. Another implication is that organizations be aware not only of negative image formation but also of how difficult it is to change that initial impression (Muthukrishnan & Chattopadhyay, 2007).

Social media is not without its critics. The third largest U.S. advertiser, General Motors, announced in early 2012 that it was dropping its $40 million Facebook campaign. While social media can reach younger consumers in a cost-effective manner, the costs cannot be justified in some industries. In the case of General Motors, the company spent over 20% of its marketing budget on digital and social media overall and will continue to offer content on Facebook (Klaman & Oreskovic, 2012). Each industry must assess its target audience and determine the most effective social media sites.

In this respect, the choice of social media can impact audiences and their perceptions of company image. Blogs seem to be the easiest foray into the world of social media for most organizations (Hale, 2010). Based within organizational web sites, they are a relatively easy way for a company to gain exposure to larger audiences and to establish itself as an expert on certain subject matter. Research has been limited on the use of blogs as a communications vehicle. Schniederjans et al. (2013) analyzed blogs, among other forms of social media, for direct assertive OIM behaviors in relation to financial rankings. While this was a quantitative study, it provided one of the few content analyses of social media in OIM research.

Some limitations in previous studies were that they measured only intent, and the products used were either fictional or nominal in price. Consequently, consumers may feel differently when faced with a monumental decision like whether to purchase legal services. The current study examined a service of significant expense, which may yield decidedly different behaviors and responses than the previous studies mentioned here. In addition, only a few studies included text and opinion mining extracted from the consumer perspective but, instead, relied on self-reported impressions and intentions.

OIM and the legal industry. Several studies have researched products or organizational image to discover best practices and perhaps examine what the uppermost performers are doing in terms of OIM. Schniederjans et al. (2013) studied OIM effects on financial performance in the pharmaceutical industry, while Chilcutt (2009) researched OIM tactics of the top performer in the airline industry. More recently, Kwok and Yu (2013) researched IM in the hospitality industry. A missing element is the examination of OIM tactics used in social media across varying industries. Following is a discussion of IM studies within the legal field.

IM studies in the legal industry. Most IM studies in the legal field have been at the individual level, examining juror perceptions of attorneys, external courtroom behavior, and verdict outcome. Attorneys and the public alike have been fixated with juries and their impression formation. Miller et al. (2010) studied IM tactics in the courtroom to see how attorney's performance and juror's perceptions of attorneys relate to final verdict. This study documented attorney performance in the areas of competence, sincerity, preparedness, opening and closing arguments, presentation of evidence, and courtroom demeanor. The sample consisted of 572 jurors from an Iowa Federal Court who filled out a questionnaire at the end of their service. The Likert questionnaire was based on two multipart statements presented to jurors at the end of the trial, which were then compared with actual jury verdict through public records. Through regression analysis, the researchers found that verdicts were related to juror's perceptions, and perceptions regarding plaintiff's attorneys were more strongly correlated with verdict outcome. Limitations included the fact that only a small number of cases were documented and that the researchers did not account for other factors that may influence impressions. Another issue was that jurors self-reported, which could have added bias. However, their findings suggested that IM was related to perceptions and outcome.

A different study on IM and law firms used the theories of Goffman (1959) as a foundation for a study on jurors (Rose et al., 2010). Rose et al. (2010) attempted to explain why jurors may form impressions based on external courthouse cues that are not formally presented in court. They analyzed 50 juries in civil trials through "offstage observations," which consisted of videotaped jury discussions and deliberations. The purpose of the study was to determine if people, atmosphere, and processes surrounding a trial can influence a jury. Observations and comments among jurors were coded by the researchers and summarized into themes. The research required special permission and elaborate security measures, along with court-ordered confidentiality limits. The findings showed that offstage encounters outside of court may alter impressions (Rose et al.,2010). However, although jurors took cues from the external environment, the study showed it played a small role in the actual deliberation process. The explanation by Rose et al. was that individuals justify events in terms consistent with their decisions; thus, juror's recollections of offstage material reinforced material they found persuasive. As these were civil cases, the study could have had a different outcome if criminal cases had been examined. The largest drawback to this research method was the need for extensive permissions from the courts to record sensitive information. Also, since the studies were conducted in a courtroom, researchers were not able to manipulate controls.

On the contrary, information *can* be controlled in social media, and variables can be measured. Therefore, what is lacking in the research on IM and law firms is the social media platform. To date, the literature regarding social media has been limited due to precautions concerning legality (Demay, 2011). Social media has fundamentally changed the landscape of business, individuals, companies, governments, privacy, and litigation issues. It has challenged attorneys in areas such as the discovery process of litigation and has posed risks in terms of reputation and unintended solicitation of legal services.

Social media and law firms. According to Demay (2011), traditional case law still applies to issues such as discoverability, but social media has once again changed the legal playing field. Demay used a number of case studies relevant to litigation raising from social media disputes. The case studies are important to consider with regard to both plaintiff's and defendant's rights. Case law is central in the study of law because of the concept of precedent. Demay's research was an overview of case law and its applicability to the use of social media, and the purpose was to demonstrate that social media has changed the landscape of litigation. Demay did not address law firms and their own use of social media. Rather, his case studies serve as a caution to abide by legal advertising standards, which include nonsolicitation of opposing parties and prohibition of "friending" under false pretenses.

Demay's case study analysis reflects on actual litigation results obtained through public records.

Demay (2011) demonstrated that law firms need to be careful how they use social media in litigation. In the future, issues, challenges, and trends will continue to emerge, and applicability of case law is still developing. While Demay cautioned attorneys against unwittingly offering legal advice online, his case studies did not research the social media of law firms. Miller et al. (2010) pointed to the number of IM studies done on juries. Most of the IM research thus far involved persuasion of juries and perceptions of attorneys and verdict. Since prior research suggests perceptions of attorneys could very well sway a verdict, IM can have significant consequences on how a legal organization is perceived by its publics.

Moreover, law firms need to be careful of the images they convey through web site content and social media. Vinson (2010) highlighted several issues law firms need to address before using electronic communications. Major issues for law firms include breach of confidentiality and posting content that could lead to allegations of representation (Vinson, 2010). However, content of electronic communications can be problematic for any organization. For example, Avery and McKay (2006) analyzed the content of corporate web sites to study visual portrayal of individuals, diversity statements, and equal employment opportunity (EEO) statements. They concluded that depicted images and other content could influence impressions of the racial or gender makeup of the company and therefore could influence recruitment efforts.

Lamertz and Martens (2011) found that law firms assisted in shaping company image and industry level risk in their study of IM of IPOs. They concluded that image constructed through professional networks showed a shared dependence and reputation by association. The image was collective among all firms. An interesting finding was that law firms not only helped shape the IPO impressions of firms, but they themselves also asserted directive dominance (Lamertz & Martens, 2011).

Financial reporting requirements can also come under scrutiny, as can disclosures (Zeller et al., 2012). Law firms traditionally oversee corporate client disclosures. Specifically, accounting disclosures in corporate narratives and press releases have gained recent attention. Organizational impression management research has been done on intentional graph manipulation or use of irrelevant comparisons (Osma & Guillamón- Saorín, 2009). While these are problems in all industries, special care must be taken by attorneys to ensure that online postings are not misconstrued as legal advice or representation.

As in other industries, law firms can also be targets of negative publicity. In a recent study by McDonnell and King (2013), firms threatened by consumer boycotts were found to engage in OIM tactics to combat negative publicity. The researchers identified publicly traded U.S. firms with a high reputational ranking on *Fortune's Most Admired Companies* list that had been covered in national newspapers over a 15-year period. McDonnell and King then analyzed the firm's responses to negative publicity via press releases. Their research showed that boycotted firms significantly increase both assertive and defensive tactics when the boycott receives more media attention and when the firm has a higher reputation (McDonnell & King, 2013). Impression management strategies were a way of counteracting negative repercussions.

Social media use by organizations has increased considerably over the past few years. It is widely used across industries and is growing among the largest revenue- producing companies. The University of Massachusetts Dartmouth Center for Marketing Research (Barnes et al., 2013) conducted a longitudinal study on the use of social media among *Fortune 500* companies. Specifically, they found most large organizations use company blogs, Facebook, Twitter, and other popular social media for their business communications. In particular, blogs were used by 34% of companies across varying industries, and at least half the companies in each industry utilized Twitter accounts. However, Facebook was by far the most popular platform, with 70% of *Fortune 500* companies utilizing it. YouTube had a 69% following, while other social media platforms accounted for less than 9% (Barnes et al., 2013). Much as others have studied *Fortune 500* companies because of their size and revenues, this study targeted the largest revenue-grossing law firms. In essence, "Due to the hugely influential role that these companies play in the business world, studying their adoption and use of social media tools offers important insights into the future of commerce" (Barnes et al., 2013, p. 1).

In recent polls conducted by the ABA, attorneys indicated that their firms had a presence in social media. However, only 59% indicated they used LinkedIn and Facebook for professional purposes. Twitter usage has increased among law firms, yet smaller and solo firms are the biggest users. These smaller firms also report getting better results with retaining clients through social media (Fairley, 2013). Law firms that ignore the impact of social media are in the minority.

The National Law Journal recently conducted a study of blog use among the top

100 law firms named in *American Lawyer Magazine* (American Lawyer, 2013; Dayton, 2013). Dayton (2013) concluded that most blog content has a leveling effect, as it is full of generic and routine information. What really mattered was the message firms send out and how they communicated it. Law firms that blogged the most were comprised of only 12 firms from the top 100 list, and together they constituted fully 46% of all blogs among the *American Lawyer* top 100 (Dayton, 2013).

Yet another study that used the 50 largest U.S. law firms from the *American Lawyer AmLaw 100* list found that while most have established a presence on social media, it is inconsistent and not used to their advantage. Researchers have found a low level of engagement as firms view social media primarily as a distribution tool for press releases. Alvarez et al. (2014) assigned point values for substantive content, reach, engagement, number of comments, likes, followers, and friends and found that law firms fall below those in other industries in terms of social media usage. Most large law firms still have an inactive presence in social media or are still in the very early stages (Alvarez et al., 2014). Alvarez et al. noted the three most popular social media platforms for law firms were Facebook, LinkedIn, and Twitter. In particular, Twitter and LinkedIn rated above Facebook in law firm usage.

Why are law firms loathe in adopting social media? The overall culture of law firms includes confidentiality, privacy, and conservatism, which directly conflict with the "disclosure culture" of social media. For this reason, law firms have been slow to adopt social media beyond company blogs. In 2009, as many as 45% of firms had blocked access or put restrictions on use of social media sites (Vinson, 2010). However, according to Dayton (2013), if firms have not embraced some form of social media by 2013, they will not remain competitive in their industries. LinkedIn has been identified as the top social network of law firms because of its reputation as a business networking site rather than a social site (LexisNexis, 2014b). Benefits from having social media include establishing the company as expert in a field of litigation; attracting clients, business opportunities, and media attention; and gathering information (Vinson, 2010). Ethical issues are still a major concern for law firms. For example, contact with witnesses, clients, adversaries, jurors, and others via social media could violate discovery rules and have other ethical consequences.

Ethical issues notwithstanding, there are legal consequences for violation of ABA rules. Online postings by those in the legal profession must be true and accurate, as they are subject to ABA Model Rule 7.1, which requires lawyers to avoid false or misleading statements (Vinson, 2010). ABA Model Rule 1.6 also prohibits disclosure of confidential information, which could be done inadvertently through social media. As noted by Vinson (2010), by publicly posting a list of contacts, a law firm may be in violation of rules of disclosure concerning client information. Further, ABA Model Rule 8.4 prohibits lawyers from engaging in conduct that is fraudulent, deceitful, dishonest, or misrepresentative. ABA Model Rule 3.6(a) prohibits attorneys from making extrajudicial statements that will be disseminated publicly where the communication has substantial likelihood of materially prejudicing a legal proceeding (Vinson, 2010). ABA Model Rule 7.3 provides additional guidance on electronic communications and prohibits lawyers from soliciting prospective clients who have previously made known that they do not want electronic communications; all such solicitations must include "advertising material" at the beginning and end of communication. Firms must also adhere to regulations regarding attorney-client relationships and unauthorized practice of law. This is only a sampling of the matters law firms must address when deciding how and when to use social media. According to Vinson (2010), social networks break down boundaries and are a very different form of communications due to increased public access and rapid spread. Law firms cannot ignore social media, but must remain cognizant of the impacts of its use (Demay, 2011).

Concluding remarks. The knowledge of understanding how the largest revenue- grossing law firms use OIM via social media tools can offer essential insights to others. Further, the findings can be a means of providing education and benchmarking for others in the legal industry (Alvarez et al., 2014). This quantitative, comparative, historical content analysis used a stratified purposive sample of law firms identified from the 2013 *American Lawyer Magazine* 100 largest revenue-grossing law firms. The independent variables were the gross annual revenues of law firms, delineated as upper and lower quartiles of the *AmLaw 100* list, and litigation specialty type. The dependent variables were the OIM strategies measured by rhetorical tone of *Optimism*, *Certainty*, *Activity*, *Realism*, and *Commonality* used in social media by the largest revenue-grossing U.S. law firms. The five values of the dependent variables are defined in Appendix C.

Further, Chapter 3 will discuss the procedure used to locate company social media per Barnes et al. (2013). After identification of the 2013 *AmLaw 100* firms, all 100 company web pages were examined for links to social media in order to identify firms active in social media. In particular, the researcher searched for firms with active Twitter sites. If none were found, a search was conducted on the company site to see if a company social media site was mentioned. If none were located, a search was conducted on Google. However, since most organizations have social media links on their web sites (Saxton & Guo, 2012), those that did not were disqualified. Content analysis was best suited to extract OIM tactics from social media for this study (Krippendorff, 2013). Further rationale for using company or industry lists, content analysis, and the OIM taxonomy in this study is discussed in the following paragraphs.

Rationale for using company or industry lists. Schniederjans et al. (2013) and Patelli and Pedrini (2013) established a positive relationship between financial performance and the use of OIM tactics in social media and other organizational communications. Financial performance is often used as a mark of successful companies, and industry rankings have become a status marker in recent years (McDonnell & King, 2013). Since several OIM studies have focused on identifying successful companies in their industries through lists from *Fortune 500, Fortune's Top 100 Employers to Work for, Most Admired Companies,* or other specific industry lists of the largest revenue- producing firms (Avery & McKay, 2006; Chilcutt, 2009; Halim & Jaafar, 2012; Kucuk, 2011; McDonnell & King, 2013; O'Keefe & Conway, 2008; Pollach & Kerbler, 2011; Westphal et al., 2012; Zeller et al., 2012), the current study explored a sample of firms from the largest revenue-grossing 100 U.S. law firms as named by *American Lawyer Magazine*.

Specific examples of past OIM studies identifying successful companies through lists include Fortune Global 500 ranking in Pollach and Kerbler's 2011 study of direct assertive IM tactics of CEO profiles on corporate web sites; a study of *Fortune 100* company's web sites (Avery & McKay, 2006) to investigate diversity in recruitment; a study of the top 200 companies in Australia for disclosure issues (Halim & Jaafar, 2012); a study of companies on the *Accredited NGOs* (non-governmental organization) list (O'Keefe & Conway, 2008); research on annual reports from corporations on the *S&P 500* lists for 7 years (Zeller et al., 2012); a study of the top profitable company in the airline industry (Chilcutt, 2009); research on negative publicity and anti-branding on the Top 100 Global Brands (Kucuk, 2011); a study of public companies with over $100 million in sales to determine the effects of IM in communications between CEOs and journalists (Westphal et al., 2012); an analysis of CEO letters and IM of the top 100 from *Fortune 500* magazine annual revenue rankings (Craig & Brennan, 2012); an analysis of *Fortune 500* companie's CEO letters across five industries (Patelli & Pedrini, 2013); a study of the effects of negative publicity on companies listed in *Fortune's Most Admired Companies* and the use of OIM tactics (McDonnell & King, 2013); and, finally, an OIM study of *S&P 500* firm's earnings and negative publicity (Tetlock et al., 2008). Each of these studies explored OIM of companies appearing on industry lists through a variety of media, including company web sites. Accordingly, this dissertation drew a sample from the list of the 2013 *American Lawyer Magazine* largest revenue-grossing U.S. law firms. A stratified random sample was used to extract six firms from the list that specialize in the areas of labor litigation, product liability, and intellectual property law. Further sampling criteria included firms that use at least two social media sites in order to identify those actively engaged in social media. Of these, the researcher located firms with active Twitter accounts. Stratified purposive sampling is often used when representation is relevant to the units from which the sample was drawn and not the entire population (Krippendorff, 2013).

Rationale for using content analysis. Prior OIM studies have used content analysis to extract IM themes from press releases, CEO letters, web sites, social media, and other forms of business communications. Pollach and Kerbler (2011) studied CEO reputations on web sites and their effects on the company. Pictorial diversity on websites was studied by Avery and McKay (2006) to extract OIM tactics in diversity and recruitment. Still other studies used content analysis to extract OIM tactics in the areas of technology and crisis communication (Vielhaber & Waltman, 2008); OIM content analysis of web sites using descriptive statistics (Huang et al., 2011); content analysis of CEO letters for defensive and assertive IM tactics (O'Keefe & Conway, 2008); OIM qualitative analysis of IPO prospectuses (Lamertz & Martens, 2011); text mining and content analysis of social media, company web sites, blogs, and forums to extract OIM tactics (Schniederjans et al., 2013); and content analysis of 18 half-hour television episodes of *Airline* to extract direct OIM assertive and defensive tactics through storylines and segments (Chilcutt, 2009). Brennan et al. (2008) used four types of content analysis approaches. Osma and Guillamón-Saorín (2009) used mixed methods to measure OIM themes in press releases and other business communications.

In summary, several prior OIM studies have used content analysis and are summarized in Appendix B. Studies similar to this research study have relied upon quantitative methods. This study attempted to examine OIM strategies of law firms via social media based on financial performance and litigation specialty type. For this reason, the study used a quantitative, comparative design with an historical content analysis data collection technique to identify OIM strategies, as measured by rhetorical tone, in social media.

Rationale for introducing the OIM taxonomy. Prior studies have shown the relevance of the tactics defined by the Mohamed et al. (1999) OIM taxonomy. However, the Mohamed et al. taxonomy is not the only OIM categorical tool used in prior research. It is mentioned in this study because it is the most prevalent tool, and research would not be complete without mention of its significance. Other researchers have studied OIM theory, but used other categorical methods. One such study was Vielhaber and Waltman's (2008) content analysis using Coomb's seven crisis response categories in which several categories overlap with OIM categories. Along the same lines, researchers Brennan et al. (2008) created a composite OIM score based on four IM methods drawn from a taxonomy of prior research on reputation and rhetorical analysis using Goffman's (1959) social influence theory (Craig & Brennan, 2012). Osma and Guillamón-Saorín (2009) used the Brennan et al. taxonomy in their mixed methods study of organizations.

Some studies used all or part of the OIM taxonomy. Pollach and Kerbler (2011) used the assertive OIM categories to study CEO profiles, which was appropriate, given that CEO profiles are intended to develop and enhance the persona of the CEO. Avery and McKay (2006) also used partial OIM taxonomy. Since hiring and recruitment focus on the presentation of organizational information, their study of press releases, web site postings, emails, and blogs focused on only direct assertive and direct defensive tactics (Avery & McKay, 2006). Yet another study used the partial OIM taxonomy of direct assertive and direct defensive tactics to analyze CEO letters of nongovernmental agencies before and after a natural disaster (O'Keefe & Conway, 2008). After negative publicity was found on the ABC news web site, O'Keefe and Conway (2008) used content analysis to see if letters contained more defensive tactics afterwards.

Even more studies have used portions of the OIM taxonomy to categorically measure oral or written verbiage, cues, and rhetorical tone. This included research by Nagy et al. (2012) linking individual IM to OIM tactics of ingratiation, self-promotion, and exemplification to determine if these tactics had an effect on the perceptions formed by stakeholders. Similarly, Tyler et al. (2012) did a study of proactive or anticipatory tactics to diffuse problematic situations. They focused on tactics of intimidation, bureaucracy, justification, and legitimacy. In Chilcutt's (2009) study of Southwest Airlines, organizational tactics achieved their precise intentions. Chilcutt studied both direct assertive and defensive tactics to see how they relate to customer satisfaction. In addition, the relationships between direct-assertive tactics in social media and financial performance were demonstrated by Schniederjans et al. (2013), who stressed the importance of building corporate image.

Summary

The study of IM has progressed from the individual to organizational behavior as a whole. While the study of IM within organizations is pervasive, little research has been conducted on OIM (Bolino et al., 2008). Few studies have been done in specific industries, such as the airline industry (Chilcutt, 2009), and several researchers have suggested that the OIM model be tested in other industries and different types of organizations (Bolino et al., 2008; Tyler et al., 2012; Vielhaber & Waltman, 2008).

More research is needed on the use of OIM strategy within social media (Schniederjans et al., 2013). Studies such as the one completed by Rose et al. (2010) show the need for more research in the area of uncontrolled cues in the courtroom, but what of controlled and uncontrolled cues in social media?

Though opening arguments, evidence, concluding statements, and nonverbal cues that influence juries and verdicts in the courtroom have been studied, research has not included OIM tactics in law via social media, even though social media has become an important platform for maintaining organizational image (Avery, 2006; Chilcutt, 2009; Schniederjans et al., 2013). Social media can increase online presence and promote success (Hale, 2010). By studying the OIM tactics of successful firms, managers and researchers can apply the OIM taxonomy to reinforce positive impressions or to minimize negative image (Chilcutt, 2009). According to Ellison, Steinfield, and Lampe (2007), online communications lack the cues of traditional communications but they are more controllable in terms of both presentation and censorship. Law firms especially have to be careful how they use OIM in social media because of legal and ethical concerns; however, those that do not understand the important role of social media will be left behind (Dayton, 2013). In summary, while extensive research has been conducted on juries and attorney impressions, none of the aforementioned studies has examined the OIM strategies of law firms in social media.

Therefore, the present quantitative study addressed the problem statement, It is not known if there are differences in social media OIM strategies based on financial performance and litigation specialty by the largest revenue-grossing U.S. law firms. The research questions were intended to answer the problem statement through an exploration of OIM strategies via social media. The research questions for this study explored the OIM strategies used by successful U.S. law firms in social media to examine differences based on annual gross revenue and litigation specialty. With the growing reliance on social media as both an advertising platform and a research tool for consumers, it has become an area that should be studied in greater detail. This research study examined the OIM tactics used by the top revenue-grossing U.S. law firms on social media sites. Chapter 3 covers the methodology and research design used in this study.

Chapter 3: Methodology

Introduction

The purpose of this causal comparative quantitative study was to examine if there were differences in social media OIM strategies based on financial performance and litigation specialty by the largest revenue-grossing U.S. law firms. Successful organizations are often identified through coveted industry lists (Bolino et al., 2008). Financial rankings have been used in prior studies as markers of successful firms (McDonnell & King, 2013). Accordingly, this study identified a sample of the largest revenue-grossing firms named in the legal industry's *American Lawyer Magazine AmLaw100*. Larger revenue-producing companies, like these, can offer important insights into emerging social media trends because of their influential role in business (Barnes et al., 2013). Therefore, this study used a stratified purposive sample of law firms from the *AmLaw 100* list to explore the OIM strategies used by financially successful law firms via social media. This chapter will elaborate on the sample criteria and social media chosen for analysis to explore the OIM strategies used by successful U.S. law firms and examine them based on revenue and litigation specialty. Moreover, Chapter 3 addresses the corresponding problem statement: It is not known if there are differences in social media OIM strategies based on financial performance and litigation specialty by the largest revenue-grossing U.S. law firms. Exploration of OIM strategies may provide insight into how successful organizations use these social media tactics to their advantage. The study results may aid in understanding how OIM can be used as a marketing tool by examining its usage in an industry bound by legal and ethical constraints. Since social media usage is rapidly growing among consumers, it is an emerging communications platform for organizations and a vehicle for OIM (Hambrick et al., 2010).

This chapter outlines the process of exploring OIM strategies through historical content analysis of social media site, Twitter. Since researchers established a link between financial performance and OIM strategies, those appearing on coveted industry lists may know how to use OIM to their advantage. This study of financially prosperous legal firms may offer insights into the use of OIM strategies via social media (Parhankangas & Ehrlich, 2012; Schniederjans et al., 2013). The following chapter outlines the research methodology.

Statement of the Problem

It is not known if there are differences in social media OIM strategies based on financial performance and litigation specialty by the largest revenue-grossing U.S. law firms. Organizational impression management is often used to achieve status and approval among industry constituents, gain public trust, and manage brand image (Saxton & Guo, 2012). Because social media is rapidly becoming an important communication vehicle for organizations (Vinson, 2010), an exploration of successful organization's OIM strategies via social media may provide guidance to those in the legal industry, as well as other organizations that need to maintain compliance with various regulatory agencies (Bobowski, 2014). Therefore, this study has added to the body of knowledge of OIM via social media within the legal industry.

Organizations, especially law firms, need to be cognizant of the impressions they convey with either presence or absence of particular content in their websites, social media, press releases, annual reports, and other communications (Pollach & Kerbler, 2011; Saxton & Guo, 2012). In other words, omission of facts can be just as demonstrative of OIM, much as intentionally placed content on external organizational communications. Previously, organizations could control image and one-way messaging, but technology has facilitated two-way external communications. Social media has the ability to rapidly cause great harm, as well as great opportunity, because of instantaneous communications from a number of sources. For example, organizational stakeholders expect quick and easily available information in response to negative publicity or an organizational crisis (Vielhaber & Waltman, 2008). Chilcutt's (2009) study of OIM strategies to combat negative publicity attested to the importance of swift company response to consumer criticism.

In addition, the study of OIM via social media has important implications since gaining public trust is critical for most organizations (Tyler et al., 2012). Companies that have appeared on coveted industry lists, such as *Fortune 500*, have earned status and reputation from their constituents (Brennan et al., 2008). Understanding how successful organizations deal with company image amid rapid, visible dissemination of communications may aid others in their marketing efforts.

Thus, OIM strategy plays a central role in formulating perceptions of company image and has particular significance for law firms that face challenges in a very competitive industry. An important consideration is that law firms are bound by legal and ethical standards in their public communications (Demay, 2011; Lamertz & Martens, 2011). An exploration of their OIM strategy may provide insight into how financially successful law firms use social media to manage organizational image within these constraints. This understanding can assist other firms with developing a set of best practices to improve or enhance public perceptions of company image.

Research Question (s) and Hypotheses

The research questions for the present study explored the OIM strategies used by successful U.S. law firms in social media and examined differences based on revenue and litigation type. This will assist in understanding what OIM strategies are used by successful U.S. law firms to manage their brand impressions via social media. The following research questions and hypotheses guided this research study and addressed the stated problem:

R1: Do differences exist in any of the five OIM strategy metrics based on revenues (bottom quartile versus top quartile)?

H1: At least one of the five OIM strategy metrics will be different based on revenue (bottom quartile versus top quartile).

H01: None of the five OIM strategy metrics will be different based on revenues (bottom quartile versus top quartile).

R2: Do differences exist in any of the five OIM strategy metrics based on specialty (labor law versus intellectual property versus product liability)? H2: At least one of the five OIM strategy metrics will be different based on specialty (labor law versus intellectual property versus product liability).

H02: None of the five OIM strategy metrics will be different based on specialty (labor law versus intellectual property versus product liability).

R3: Do differences exist in any of the five OIM strategy metrics based on year (2010 through 2014)?

H3: At least one of the five OIM strategy metrics will be different based on year (2010 through 2014).

H03: None of the five OIM strategy metrics will be different based on year (2010 through 2014).

The independent variables were gross annual revenues of law firms, delineated as upper and lower quartiles of the *AmLaw 100* list, and litigation specialty type. The dependent variables were the OIM strategies measured by rhetorical tone of *Optimism, Certainty, Activity, Realism,* and *Commonality* used in social media by the largest revenue-grossing U.S. law firms. The five dependent variables are defined in Appendix C. Diction has five Master Variables that are comprised of the dependent variables in this study. Prior OIM studies have related four of the five Master Variables to OIM strategies. For example, *Optimism, Certainty, Realism,* and *Commonality* have been tied to OIM strategy (Craig & Brennan, 2012; Craig et al., 2013; Patelli & Pedrini, 2013; Schniederjans et al., 2013).

To answer the research questions and test the hypotheses, this study required a quantitative, causal comparative design. The research questions called for between groups analysis of numerical variables. The data sources were public financial records of law firm rankings and publicly available organizational social media sites. The largest U.S. revenue-grossing law firms were identified through the annual *AmLaw 100* list published by *American Lawyer Magazine*. A stratified purposive sample of law firms fitting the criteria described in the next section was identified by the researcher.

The researcher analyzed the social media sites of the sample as follows. First, the researcher examined company websites. According to LexisNexis (2014a), law firms that demonstrate commitment to social media connect their web site home pages to various networks such as Twitter, Facebook, and LinkedIn. The method used to identify social media usage in this study mirrored that of Barnes et al. (2013), who identified a sample from the *Fortune 500* list of highest revenue-grossing firms. Likewise, company web sites were identified for this study by working through the list of the *AmLaw 100* largest revenue-grossing law firms. Next, litigation specialty was noted through web site content. Following Barnes et al., social media sites of firms were identified first through examining company web pages for links or mention of social media. If none were listed, a search was done on the company's web site, which proved to be an effective method for

Barnes et al. Therefore, social media was located by examining the company web site.

This study identified firms that use two forms of social media to locate those actively engaged in social media communications. Blogs and Twitter were named as the fastest-growing social media used by both public and private companies (Barnes et al.,2013). Twitter was identified as one of two most widely used social media platform by law firms in the past few years, along with LinkedIn (LexisNexis, 2014b). Twitter traditionally has had more frequent and varied content than organizational LinkedIn pages. Therefore, firms selected for the present study had to utilize Twitter as part of their social media communications. Twitter has gained popularity with a decidedly different demographic than traditional social media users, which are teenagers and college students. The "unparalleled explosion in popularity" of Twitter among adults can be attributed to its use for professional purposes (Miller, 2009, p. 1). These include Twitter's ability to rapidly broadcast ideas, follow news, network with industry contacts, and market products and brands in an efficient manner (Miller, 2009).

Twitter was also found to be number one among social media for *Fortune 500* firms in 2012-2013 (Barnes et al., 2013). Seventy-seven percent of *Fortune 500* companies have Twitter accounts and have tweeted within the past thirty days. Twitter is the leading social media site for advertising, PR and marketing, even among non-profits (Lovejoy et al., 2012). Moreover, social networking is "explosive" in the legal field (Vinson, 2010, p. 356). Therefore, Twitter was chosen for analysis in this study because of (a) its popularity among law firms on the most current *AmLaw 100* list (b) the volume of tweets far exceeds content in LinkedIn and blogs, and (c) because it is one of the fastest-growing and most effective social media platforms for organizations (Miller, 2009). For these reasons, Twitter was an appropriate social media choice for this study.

After identification of the sample, data from Twitter was downloaded and prepared for textual analysis. Tweets from each firm's Twitter account were organized in descending chronological order extending back 5 years from the present. Tweets were downloaded from years 2014, 2013, 2012, 2011, and 2010 per law firm. The data was entered into a spreadsheet and organized by company, specialty type, annual revenues, dates, and number of tweets.

Research Methodology

This study used a quantitative methodology and a causal comparative research design to examine OIM strategies in social media based on financial performance and litigation specialty (Gravetter & Wallnau, 2013). An overwhelming number of prior OIM studies have used qualitative, quantitative, or mixed-methods methodologies (Avery & McKay, 2006; Bravo et al., 2012; Brennan et al., 2008; Chilcutt, 2009; Craig & Brennan, 2012; Hall et al., 2013; Lamertz & Martens, 2011; McDonnell & King, 2013; O'Keefe & Conway, 2008; Osma & Guillamón-Saorín, 2009; Patelli & Pedrini, 2013; Pollach & Kerbler, 2011; Schniederjans et al., 2013; Huang et al., 2011; Tyler et al., 2012; Vielhaber & Waltman, 2008). The methodologies used in prior OIM studies are listed in Appendix B. Whether they were quantitative or qualitative was highly dependent upon the research question. Prior OIM studies used qualitative research for descriptive analysis, whereas correlational studies used quantitative methodology. The use of quantitative methodology examines data in terms of numbers and causal or correlational relationships (Krippendorff, 2013).

Accordingly, the intent of this study was to examine if there were differences in social media OIM strategies of successful U.S. law firms based on financial performance and litigation specialty. Therefore, quantitative methodology was appropriate. Although social media is a rich resource for organizational communications (Hale, 2010), thus ripe for qualitative research, a qualitative study was not the most suitable method for answering the research questions. The research questions required quantitative analysis to properly assess the differences among law firms in terms of annual gross revenue and litigation specialty. As such, the variables in this study were quantifiable in nature and were measured using a validated measurement tool.

In summary, this study examined the data through a quantitative, causal comparative design utilizing an historical content analysis to explore the differences between measurable variables. The dependent variables, OIM strategies measured through rhetorical tone, were examined in light of the independent variables of annual gross revenues and litigation specialty.

Research Design

This was a quantitative methodological study using a causal comparative design, with an historical content analysis on a stratified purposive sample of law firms. A quantitative causal comparative study design was needed in order to examine the OIM strategies in social media based on financial performance and litigation specialty. Causal comparative design was chosen over predictive correlational, cross-sectional, experimental, or other quantitative designs since the purpose of this study was to examine differences in social media OIM strategy based on two variables, annual gross revenues and litigation specialty. Thus, the statistical analysis for this study was a between-groups design using repeated measures ANOVA, and this required a causal comparative research design (Devlin, 2006).

First, the data for this analysis was historical. Historical design requires that something has occurred, was said, or was printed in the past in order to be classified through content analysis (Krippendorff, 2013). This study used an historical analysis of social media sites of a stratified purposive sample of law firms. It used publicly available data posted on firm's social media sites for analysis of OIM themes. Using historical data, Pollach and Kerbler (2011) did similar content analysis studies of CEO profiles on corporate web sites. Chilcutt (2009) performed a historical content analysis of OIM strategies used in television episodes. In the current study, social media communications were collected through an historical analysis of company postings. Historical data beginning from the present working backwards was downloaded until a sufficient number of social media postings were amassed for each firm for the years 2010 through 2014. In keeping with prior correlational OIM research, the present study examined data through a quantitative causal comparative design, with an historical content analysis of OIM tactics used in social media (Kwok, 2012).

Second, the research questions were best answered through a causal comparative design. Other designs considered were qualitative in nature. Case studies, ethnographies, narratives, and phenomenological studies are more suited for longitudinal studies and exploratory research of themes or patterns. Conversely, this study attempted to examine OIM strategies via social media, as measured by rhetorical tone, based on financial revenue and litigation specialty. Other correlational designs, such as predictive or experimental were not considered for this study, since a causal comparative design was sufficient to answer the research questions. The present study did not seek to predict outcomes, nor was it experimental in nature through manipulation of variables. The study attempted to explore the OIM strategies of successful firms to determine if differences exist based on annual gross revenues and litigation specialty type.

Third, the data for causal comparative analysis was downloaded from each firm's Twitter site, run through computerized content analysis, and quantified. The use of content analysis was best for extracting data from organizational communications, such as social media. Content analysis has been used to explore organizational communications in the form of pictorals, such as graphs, web sites, and other visuals, and also to extract linguistic characteristics such as semantics and rhetorical tone (Avery & McKay, 2006; Barnes et al., 2013; Brennan et al., 2008; Chilcutt, 2009; Lamertz & Martens, 2011; O'Keefe & Conway, 2008; Osma & Guillamón-Saorín, 2009; Parhankangas & Ehrlich, 2012; Pollach & Kerbler, 2011; Schniederjans et al., 2013; Huang et al., 2011; Vielhaber & Waltman, 2008). These prior studies are summarized in Appendix B. The current research study used rhetorical tone to measure OIM strategies in social media. Therefore, a quantitative causal comparative design was best to answer the research questions for this study. In summary, the research questions posed by this study necessitated a quantitative study using a causal comparative design and a stratified purposive sample of law firms (Krippendorff, 2013). A purposive sample was drawn from the *American Lawyer* annual list of the 100 largest revenue-grossing law firms to represent firms that are U.S.-based, specialize in different types of litigation, and specifically use Twitter.

Population and Sample Selection

Each year, legal industry publication *American Lawyer Magazine* lists the largest law firms, both globally and nationally, in terms of revenue, volume, number of attorneys, and other criteria. Law firms provide their financials voluntarily and are independently investigated by the publication. Financial rankings are by *gross revenue* per firm, defined as fee income from legal work only, not including income or disbursements from nonlegal ancillary activity (American Lawyer, 2013).

Population. The population under study was the *AmLaw 100* list of largest revenue-producing U.S. law firms. This population was chosen because firms have been selected by their constituents to appear on a coveted industry list. Selection for the *AmLaw 100* is done by an assembly of peers who monitor the largest U.S. law firms and most accomplished attorneys (American Lawyer, 2013). Organizations in prior OIM studies have been identified as appearing on coveted lists, such as *Fortune 500* or other rankings (Avery & McKay, 2006; Barnes et al., 2013; Chilcutt, 2009; Halim & Jaafar, 2012 ; Kucuk, 2011; McDonnell & King, 2013; O'Keefe & Conway, 2008; Patelli & Pedrini, 2013; Pollach & Kerbler, 2011; Westphal et al., 2012; Zeller et al., 2012). Appearance on industry lists is a goal for which many organizations strive since it has become a reputational vehicle and status marker for them. This goal is often reached through carefully crafted images and public communications through the use of OIM strategies (McDonnell & King, 2013). Since prior research has focused on strategies of successful firms within other industries, this research study may provide insight into OIM social media strategies of successful law firms.

Sample. A stratified purposive sample was used to extract six firms from the 100 largest revenue-grossing law firms in the United States, as named by *American Lawyer Magazine*. Historical data was retrieved from March 2014 in reverse chronological order until there were at least 500 messages for each firm from the social media site, Twitter, for the years 2010 through 2014.

Collection of data from six firms over a period of 5 years, at minimum 500 messages per year, yielded 15,000 messages for units of analysis. It was assumed that Twitter messages, although relegated to 140 characters, would occur more frequently and thus produce greater volume of posts in general. For example, organizations post fewer words in Twitter, but the volume of messages can be greater (Mathioudakis & Koudas, 2010).

Alternatively, organizational blogs vary in content and thus were not considered for this study. Some firms produce more data and more frequent content than others. Some organizations typically have a number of themed blogs, while others have one or two posts. For example, a general litigation firm may have different blogs categories of product liability, medical malpractice, employment issues, and environmental concerns.

Blogs are not limited in length, but are left to each organization's discretion. Thus, organizational blogs were not used in this study.

Similarly, LinkedIn was not chosen for this study because it typically does not contain as much data as other social media. LinkedIn is a tool that companies use to showcase their talents and summarize key points. LinkedIn data are inherently brief in nature. Also, LinkedIn information is usually only available for the past 30-90 days. For that reason, this study did not use LinkedIn "postings" as the social media analysis of law firms.

Due to the differences in volume generated by different law firms, word count

was used as the smallest unit of information (Krippendorff, 2013). As such, over 160,000 words were analyzed in total. Krippendorff (2013) stated that in order to obtain reliable accounts of larger units, many content analysts have relied upon smaller units, such as words, to ensure agreement in describing text. For example, if the average word length is 4-6 characters (Hart, 2014), gathering the minimum stated 500 *tweets* at 140 characters, would yield 14,000 words per firm. However, close to 10,000 *tweets* totaling over 160,000 words were analyzed in this study.

Lastly, selection of the sample was considered purposive since it was chosen from a relatively small population of the 100 largest revenue-grossing U.S. law firms. The purpose was to study the OIM strategies of this particular group of successful firms, excluding the larger population of law firms in general. Purposive sampling is often used when representation is relevant to the units from which the sample was drawn and not the entire population (Krippendorff, 2013).

Stratification. Further criteria were included to accommodate strata, or subgroups, that are representative of the larger population (Krippendorff, 2013). In order to account for differences in specialty areas, an equal number of firms was selected to represent product liability litigation, intellectual property law, and employment and labor law. To further retain financial objectivity, firms were chosen equally from the upper and lower quartiles of the list. In stratified purposive sampling, the researcher follows a conceptual hierarchy, thus systematically decreasing the quantity fitting criteria for analysis (Krippendorff, 2013). The information required to narrow the sample selection was from publicly available data through *AmLaw 100* financial lists and from company web sites. Thus, data collected on annual gross revenues and litigation specialties of the sample firms served as the independent variables for the present study.

The remaining criteria for this study were that the selected sample use social media, which was central to this study. The most popular external social media sites for law firms are Twitter and LinkedIn (LexisNexis, 2014b). An initial review of the *AmLaw 100* public organizational web sites confirmed the popularity of both, with Twitter as the most popular social media platform of these firms. Results are reflected in Table 5.

Table 5. Social Media Use by Legal Firms on the AmLaw 100 List

Social Media	Number of Firms
Facebook	42
Twitter	59

LinkedIn	55
Google	24
Blogs	13
None	29

Exclusions. Of the top 100 revenue-grossing law firms, five were disqualified because they were defined as *vereins* (non-U.S.-based firms) per the American Bar Association. Secondly, those without social media sites were also exempt since the intent of this study was to research OIM via social media. Social media usage was further identified through law firm's web pages per Barnes et al. (2013). For example, an initial review of public web sites revealed that none of the *merger and acquisition* specialty firms had social media sites. Hence, that specialty litigation group was omitted from this sample. Even if they added social media before the conclusion of this study, it is doubtful there would have been enough data to collect.

Initial review of public organizational web sites. Of the seven firms identified as labor law, five have social media sites; 10 of 12 firms devoted solely to intellectual property law have social media sites; 6 of 8 product liability specialty firms have social media sites. All others are general litigation firms. Most firms have Twitter and/or LinkedIn. Therefore, the final sample consisted of six firms within the specialties of labor law, product liability, and intellectual property law that use social media site Twitter. The messages within Twitter, known as *tweets*, became the units of analysis for the sample.

Confidentiality measures. As noted earlier, financials are voluntarily provided by law firms appearing on the *AmLaw 100* list and are verified by *American Lawyer* investigators (American Lawyer, 2013). The financial data and rankings are publicly available information. As such, this study did not require an informed consent process or participation requirements. The rankings are available on the Internet and include both U.S. and global firms. This study used the U.S. law firm rankings of the largest 100 revenue-grossing firms available at www.americanlawyer.com. Confidentiality measures in this study included coding the sample inasmuch as individual law firms will not be named in the study.

Instrumentation

The present study used two established quantitative instruments. First, it relied upon publicly available information from reputable sources that provided the data for analysis. Information from public sources that provides data about a population or sample is considered a quantitative instrument (Neuendorf, 2002). Second, this study used a valid, reliable, and consistent measurement tool for the analysis of rhetorical tone. Both are discussed in the following sections.

Independent variables. The initial set of data was gathered from public financial records and rankings of law firms from the annual *American Lawyer Magazine* list of largest revenue-grossing firms. The data came from a respected source in the legal industry. Financials are voluntarily submitted and verified through independent investigation. *American Lawyer Magazine* gross revenue rankings are based on fee income from legal work only, excluding disbursements and income from nonlegal ancillary businesses (American Lawyer, 2013). To be included in the study, firms had to be U.S. based, have a litigation specialty area for objectivity of specialty type, and use social media. Therefore, the first independent variable, gross annual revenue, was collected from the *AmLaw 100* list.

The second independent variable, litigation specialty type, also came from publicly available data. Litigation specialty type is usually listed along with firm data on the *AmLaw 100* list. However, the researcher verified litigation specialty through cultivation of public, online news articles, journals, and other public postings regarding firm descriptions. The litigation specialty types that were used in the current study were labor law, intellectual property law, and product liability law. Although a vast majority of the *AmLaw 100* practices general litigation, many firms are known for their specialty in one major litigation area.

Dependent variables. The dependent variables for this study were the OIM strategies, measured in rhetorical tone, of law firm's social media sites. The five rhetorical tone variables are defined as *Optimism, Certainty, Activity, Realism,* and *Commonality*. These were measured through a validated instrument that has been used in prior OIM research. The dependent variables were analyzed through repeated measures ANOVA in SPSS to examine differences among firms, based on annual gross revenue and litigation specialty.

Measurement. An instrument may be defined as a tool for measuring, observing, or documenting quantitative data (Neuendorf, 2002). One such measurement tool successfully used in prior OIM studies is a computerized content analysis program, Diction, which measures rhetorical tone on a wide variety of organizational communications. Diction was used to measure rhetorical tone among five variables (independent variables): *Optimism, Certainty, Activity, Realism,* and *Commonality*. Appendix C offers definitions for these variables. Rhetorical tone has been measured in prior studies and has been used effectively to measure OIM strategies (Craig & Brennan, 2012; Craig et al., 2013; Hall et al., 2013; Parhankangas & Ehrlich, 2012; Patelli & Pedrini, 2013). The researcher interpreted the measurement scores to analyze OIM strategies apparent on firm's social media sites. Diction is discussed further in the following section in terms of reliability, validity, and consistency.

Validity

Validity is defined as the degree to which a test measures what it is assumed and intended to measure (Gravetter & Wallnau, 2013). A common method for determining validity is the use of correlation to assess how well a test holds compared to previous measures of the same item (Krippendorff, 2013). Thus, an acceptable method of determining validity is to examine prior studies that have used the same measurement instrument.

Following prior OIM research, the present study used Diction's five master variables to measure rhetorical tone in law firm's social media (Craig & Brennan, 2012; Hall et al., 2013; Patelli & Pedrini, 2013). Use of coding dictionaries is an acceptable practice for both qualitative and quantitative content analysis, and the steps are easily replicable (Krippendorff, 2013). The notion that computer searches mask interpretations and meanings is refuted by Krippendorff (2013), who stated that the queries and searches are formulated by analysts who, in turn, interpret the results. The theory behind dictionary approaches "derives from taxonomy, the idea that texts can be represented on different levels of abstraction, or that there are core meanings and insignificant variations of these cores" (Krippendorff, 2013, p. 239). For web-based analysis, software coding is a functional way of processing data due to its speed and efficiency in handling a large volume of data (Neuendorf, 2002). The following section discusses the types of validity that were considered for this study.

Functional validation. Researchers can assess a dictionary's functional validity if it has been found to measure what it was intended to measure based on how successfully it has been used in the past (Krippendorff, 2013). The dictionary used in this study was the *Corporate Public Relations* normative dictionary within the analysis tool. Diction software has been used in prior OIM studies with success (Craig & Brennan, 2012; Hall et al., 2013; Patelli & Pedrini, 2013). Therefore, as a tool for analysis, Diction has functional validity. Further, some researchers have tied rhetorical tone, as measured by this software, to the categories in the OIM taxonomy (Avery & McKay, 2006; Chilcutt, 2009; Nagy et al., 2012; O'Keefe & Conway, 2008; Pollach & Kerbler, 2011; Schniederjans et al., 2013; Tyler et al., 2012; Vielhaber & Waltman, 2008).

The use of Diction content analysis software was appropriate for this study because of its unique ability to extract rhetorical tone and meaning from otherwise meaningless words and phrases. Text invariably has latent connotations, and readers are often create their interpretations, as "texts inevitably have multiple meanings"(Krippendorff, 2013, p. 357). Rhetorical tone analysis has been successfully used since the 1960s to assess content in speeches, documents, and countless corporate communications media.

Semantic validation. *Semantic validity* refers to the extent the categories in analysis correspond to the meanings these texts have to readers within a chosen context (Krippendorff, 2013). Use of software also offers semantic validity, the extent to which persons familiar with the language agree that the text has similar meanings or connotations. Semantic validity is often dependent on coder's subject matter knowledge, experience, and agreement (Krippendorff, 2013). The normative database used in this study runs textual analysis against more than 50,000 texts from a variety of sectors, including politics, law, business, science, fiction, and media. In addition, researchers can choose to analyze text from specific categories, such as "corporate business communications," that have been validated in other studies. According to Krippendorff (2013), a prerequisite for the use of software is that it has been semantically validated through prior use. Dictionaries are based on semantic theory and, thus, avoid intercoder reliability problems caused by subjectivity (Patelli & Pedrini, 2013). This study used the normative database of "corporate business communications" as the method of analysis for studying organizational communications via social media (Hart, 2014).

Sampling validity. The population under study was from *American Lawyer Magazine's* 100 largest revenue-grossing U.S. firms list. Firms and their financials appearing on this list have been verified as accurate by industry experts (American Lawyer, 2013). A subset of this population was identified through criteria specified in previous sections. The *AmLaw 100* population was chosen since other successful organizations have been identified from coveted industry lists in prior OIM studies, such as *Fortune 500, Most Admired Companies, Best Companies to Work For,* and *Inc. 500* (Avery & McKay, 2006; Barnes et al., 2013; Chilcutt, 2009; Halim & Jaafar, 2012; Kucuk, 2011; McDonnell & King, 2013; O'Keefe & Conway, 2008; Patelli & Pedrini,

2013; Pollach & Kerbler, 2011; Westphal et al., 2012; Zeller et al., 2012). The findings from the analysis of the sample may be generalized to the population of the *AmLaw 100* U.S. law firms. In addition, other law firms and organizations can use the information to gain insight as to how successful firms use OIM via social media for organizational advantage.

Content validity. Krippendorff (2013) defined *content validity* as the extent that the study captures all the features that define the concept. The concept in the current study was measurement of rhetorical tone in organizational social media. Rhetorical tone has been tied to OIM (Avery & McKay, 2006; Chilcutt, 2009; Nagy et al., 2012; O'Keefe & Conway, 2008; Pollach & Kerbler, 2011; Schniederjans et al., 2013; Tyler et al., 2012; Vielhaber & Waltman, 2008). This robustness indicates empirical validity, while automated analysis warrants measurement validity (Patelli & Pedrini, 2013). In summary, the body of literature supports use of Diction software to measure rhetorical tone since it has been used and validated in a number of prior OIM studies.

Internal and external validity. This study is reflective of a passive design, meaning there was no manipulation of variables. Firms types, annual gross revenues, and Twitter postings have already been established. Often referred to as quasi-experimental research, this design offers greater external validity for generalization to external populations (Devlin, 2006). In addition, the use of a validated measurement tool, Diction, can control for internal validity.

Reliability

Reliability refers to accuracy, replicability, and stability. Problems that can arise concerning reliability are intra-observer disagreement, individual inconsistencies, and coding errors (Krippendorff, 2013). The use of content analysis software may be of more assurance that the test will be reliable, as it will not rely on the subjective judgments of the researcher (Neuendorf, 2002; Saldana, 2009).

Stability. *Stability* is defined as the degree to which the process remains unchanged over time (Krippendorff, 2013). Krippendorff (2013) stated that reliable data remain constant throughout the measurement process. Data stability could be a problem as organizations frequently update and change their web sites and other social media content. However, general themes and content would not vary as much due to the nature of intended portrayals of company image. In the present study, data stability was ensured because the researcher used historical content on social media sites that was chronologically logged, posted, and unchanged. In addition, built-in dictionaries assure stability in textual analysis (Hart, 2014). In contrast, stability is tested in manual coding by using two or more researchers where there may be inconsistencies (Krippendorff, 2013). In software-assisted coding, stability is generated through use of the same dictionaries and taxonomies over time and studies.

Replicability. The use of software programs to extract content makes this study highly replicable. According to Krippendorff (2013), the use of dictionaries enhances this process. In addition, as more studies use the same dictionaries, the outcomes become more reliable. The present study utilized computer-based dictionaries used in prior OIM research to analyze rhetorical tone in social media.

Accuracy. According to Krippendorff (2013), *accuracy* is the degree to which the

process conforms to its specifications and the produces for which it is designed. In manual analysis, the problems with accuracy stem from intracoder disagreements, deviation from standards, and individual inconsistencies. With software analysis, replicability and accuracy are based on the number of researchers using the same analysis programs. However, since interpretations may be complex, accuracy standards may suffer when using software (Krippendorff, 2013). To account for this possibility, the researcher further interpreted the data.

In summary, the use of the same tool to measure rhetorical tone as other OIM studies contributes to its strong empirical validity and reliability (Patelli & Pedrini, 2013). The five master variables (independent variables) have gone through multicollinearity tests indicating statistical independence of each variable from another (Patelli & Pedrini, 2013). Three types of reliability are (a) stability, where analysis remains unaffected over time; (b) reproducibility, the degree to which the study can be recreated; and (c) accuracy, the degree the study design conforms to standards (Brennan et al., 2008).

Through use of the same measurement tool that has been used in prior OIM research, this study maintained stability, reproducibility, and accuracy.

Data Collection Procedures

Data was collected from public sources, such as web sites, social media sites, and public financial records from a sample of the 100 largest revenue-grossing U.S. law firms. The list of the largest revenue-grossing law firms identified from the *American Lawyer Magazine* 2013 annual report, mirrors prior OIM studies that have also focused on identifying the largest revenue-grossing companies in their industries (Avery & McKay, 2006; Barnes et al.,

2013; Chilcutt, 2009; Halim & Jaafar, 2012; Kucuk, 2011; McDonnell & King, 2013; O'Keefe & Conway, 2008; Pollach & Kerbler, 2011; Schniederjans et al., 2013; Westphal et al., 2012; Zeller et al., 2012). This population was chosen because these firm's appearance on a coveted industry list denotes status and financial success among industry peers and constituents (McDonnell & King, 2013). The list is publicly available, published online and in print in several publications throughout the U.S. (American Lawyer, 2013).

Use of public data. In addition, these publications include select financial records of law firms that appear on the list, such as gross revenues, earnings per share, earnings per partner, and so forth. Social media sites, including LinkedIn, Twitter, and company web blogs, are also public material. As such, there were no privacy violations or need for informed consent for participation in this study.

Procedure for identification/collection of social media data. Last and most important, firms fitting the criteria were checked for social media usage, which was central to this study. *Social media* can be defined as electronic communications through Web 2.0 platforms, which includes web sites, community forums, LinkedIn, Twitter, Facebook, Google, blogs, YouTube, web portals, news groups, and discussion boards (Hale, 2010; Hambrick et al., 2010). The most popular forms of social media for law firms are Twitter, LinkedIn, and company blogs (LexisNexis, 2014b). In turn, the most popular social media for firms on the current *AmLaw 100* list is Twitter (Table 5). Therefore, data was collected from Twitter's public social media sites.

The present study followed the procedure for data collection used by Barnes et al. (2013). The researcher identified social media sites of firms through examination of company web pages for links or mention of social media in order to find firms that are active in social media. If none were listed, a search was done on the company's web site, which proved to be an effective method for Barnes et al. According to LexisNexis (2014a), law firms that demonstrate commitment to social media connect their web site home pages to various networks such as Twitter, Facebook, and LinkedIn. Therefore, in the present study, two forms of social media, including Twitter, were located by examining the company website. It should be noted that some companies use social media tools (e.g., employee blogs) internally rather than publicly. Barnes et al. (2013) did not count these as public social media, and neither did this researcher. Although law firm's websites were searched for active social media usage, only Twitter was used for analysis in the present study.

Collection of organizational posts. After identification of company social media, the researcher downloaded the data with specialty browser software found in the

program, *NVivo*. Data collected included organizational postings on the Twitter pages of each firm. Historical data was retrieved from March 2014 in reverse chronological order for 5 years through the year 2010 for each firm. Some firms may have started using social media only recently, while others have used it for several years. Data were assigned eight alphanumeric identifiers that are unique to each firm's social media and year. The identifiers, discussed later in this chapter, were used to mark type of social media, dates, number of units, and other markers that may be tracked to control for firm differences.

It was expected that social media would provide robust data. Indeed, the Twitter messages per firm over a 5-year period yielded an analysis of at least 10,000 units. *Units* are defined as identifiable messages drawn from the sample upon which variables are measured (Neuendorf, 2002). While there are no universally accepted criteria for selecting sample size in content analysis, higher numbers of units would guarantee more meaningful results. Neuendorf (2002) used an example from 52 issues of weekly newspapers, concluding that 1,067 headlines would be sufficient for a 99% confidence interval (pp. 89-91). As such, the current study had enough units for a 95% confidence interval. According to Krippendorff (2013), an appropriate sample size has been reached when the researcher has an adequate number of messages to answer the research questions.

Twitter data, for example, can run up to thousands of messages and remain posted for years. In contrast, LinkedIn pages hold minimal data that is stored for a short period of time, and organizational blogs, while lengthy, are often less frequently posted. The current study used Twitter rather than blogs or LinkedIn simply because of the volume of short posts in Twitter greatly exceeds that of other social media. With Twitter, however, over 160,000 words were analyzed for this study.

Thus, the data collected from social media site, Twitter, was used to identify the dependent variables. The dependent variables were OIM strategies measured through rhetorical tone of *Optimism*, *Certainty*, *Activity*, *Realism*, and *Commonality*. They are defined in Appendix C. This causal comparative study examined if there were any differences in the dependent variables based on the independent variables, gross annual revenues and specialty.

Data security. All data collected for this study are publicly available information. It should be noted that the law firms selected for the sample were coded for anonymity and not individually named in the study. The reasonable and customary length of time to keep records for most professions is 5 years. A *reasonable and customary amount of time* is defined as common socially acceptable practice; as such, there is no specific definition. For example, student academic material kept by professors and real estate transactional records kept by brokers are to be maintained for 5 years in the state of Arizona.

Following this generalization, the records from the present study will be kept by the researcher on the researcher's personal computer for at least 5 years.

After that time, electronic data will be expunged, and paper copies, if any, will be shredded.

Data Analysis Procedures

The research questions for the present study explored what OIM strategies are used by successful U.S. law firms in social media and examined differences based on revenue and litigation type. Historical content analysis has been used in prior OIM research to measure word frequencies, rhetorical tone, visual cues, semantics, and other language features (Brennan et al., 2008; Chilcutt, 2009; Tetlock et al., 2008). For example, Tetlock et al. (2008) quantified language in newspaper articles to measure OIM tactics. For the purpose of this study, OIM strategies were measured through rhetorical tone.

Repeated measures ANOVA is considered a robust statistical technique that allows for explanations caused by other variables, such as annual gross revenue and litigation specialty type (Devlin, 2006). It also provides for interaction effect among variables. Since the researcher is interested in interaction effects, repeated measures ANOVA was the correct statistical procedure for this study to control for Type I error, rejection of the null hypothesis if it is true. A repeated measures ANOVA was used to determine size, interaction effect, and direction between the independent variables and dependent variables. The independent variables were tested for normalcy through a Shapiro-Wilks test, visual inspections of graphs, and tested for skewness and kurtosis (Gravetter & Wallnau, 2013). A repeated measure ANOVA was the appropriate test to determine relationships between the independent and dependent variables (Krippendorff, 2013).

The variables for this study were continuous; therefore, any missing data may be replaced by a numerical mean of that item up to a third of the data without changing the study outcome (Devlin, 2006). It was anticipated that there was a sufficient number of tweets per firm to allocate into batches according to date. Indeed, ANOVA also allows for different sized samples, in the event some firms had greater volume of *tweets* than others (Gravetter & Wallnau, 2013).

Data. Data for the present study was retrieved through the procedures mentioned in the previous section. Annual gross revenue and specialty type for this quantitative, causal comparative study were collected from publicly available information on *AmLaw 100* law firms. Annual gross revenue and litigation specialty served as the independent variables in this study.

Data for the dependent variables was collected from organizational postings on the social media site, Twitter. The dependent variables, *Optimism, Certainty, Activity, Realism,* and *Commonality* were measured through software that has been employed in previous OIM studies (Bravo et al., 2012;

Brennan et al., 2008; Craig & Brennan, 2012; Craig et al., 2013; Hall et al., 2013; Parhankangas & Ehrlich, 2012; Patelli & Pedrini, 2013). Thus, the body of literature supports the use of content analysis software for data analysis, since it has been validated in a number of prior OIM studies. In contrast, manual coding is labor-intensive and subject to criticism due to subjectivity, low reliability, and low validity (Brennan et al., 2008).

Preparation of data. Social media requires specialty software to download content, especially if it contains large files, extensive content, or multimedia. The present study used *NVivo* web browser extensions to capture data on company social media sites. The data was prepared for input and textual content analysis into Diction software. Once the data from social media sites was downloaded into spreadsheet format, the researcher converted the data into .txt format. This involved scrubbing the data of all non-textual content, such as visuals and hashtags. Although Diction can read a variety of formats, .txt files are preferred. The verbal content of social media was prepared in .txt format and assigned eight identifiers. These identifiers were assigned by the researcher to code (a) organizations, (b) social media type, (c) posting dates, (d) number of posts, (e) litigation specialty, (f) financial ranking, and a (g) unique alphanumeric ID. The alphanumeric ID was assigned for organizational anonymity. Rhetorical tone was measured on the variables *Optimism*, *Certainty*, *Activity*, *Realism*, and *Commonality*. The variables are defined in Appendix C.

According to Patelli and Pedrini (2013), prior studies lack comprehensive measurement, which reduces their validity. To overcome this challenge, Diction software has been used to measure rhetorical tone as an OIM strategy (Bravo et al., 2012; Brennan et al., 2008; Craig & Brennan, 2012; Craig et al., 2013; Hall et al., 2013; Parhankangas & Ehrlich, 2012; Patelli & Pedrini, 2013). Diction 7.0 is the newest version of a linguistic analysis program that uses several dictionaries based on five master variables: (a) Certainty, (b) Optimism, (c) Activity, (d) Realism, and (e) Commonality (Hart, 2014). The *Certainty* category indicates resoluteness, inflexibility, completeness, and honesty. The *Optimism* category indicates highlights of accomplishments, endorsements, or positive verbiage. The *Activity* category captures movement, change, and innovations. The *Realism* category refers to descriptions of tangible, current, and immediate matters. Lastly, the *Commonality* category indicates emphasis on group values.

In addition to the five master variables, nearly 40 categories of other variables relate to themes and rhetorical tone of texts. These are described in Appendix C. Through use of Diction, as evidenced in prior OIM research, this study maintained stability, reproducibility, and accuracy in answering the research questions.

Diction relies on a vast array of dictionaries and prior empirical studies across different industries and compares the results of text analysis to a "normal range of scores" that has been developed through comparison of more than

50,000 texts (Patelli & Pedrini, 2013). Scores are converted to z-scores with the standard deviation +/- 1 (Hart, 2014). Raw scores are often converted to z-scores to make data more meaningful and make comparisons more accurate (Gravetter & Wallnau, 2013). A common reason for using z-scores is to standardize a distribution for equal comparison among tests. The z-scores in Diction are arrived through a combination of subtraction and addition of sub-variables and adding a constant of 50 for elimination of negative numbers (Hart, 2014).

Although Diction began as an analysis tool for political speeches, its use has since expanded to include a multitude of corporate communications. Diction has often been used to analyze corporate narratives, CEO letters, political speeches, and other types of organizational communications (Craig et al., 2013). The dictionary is based on a collection of such narratives reaching back to the 1960s. This robustness indicates empirical validity, while automated analysis warrants measurement validity (Patelli & Pedrini, 2013).

Software coding was chosen for content analysis in this study because of its ability to quickly and objectively code large amounts of data (Pang & Lee, 2008). Manual coding is labor-intensive and subject to criticism due to subjectivity, low reliability, and low validity (Brennan et al., 2008). Diction can account for differences between long and short passages for similar measurement of text (Hart, 2014). In this study, differences can arise from higher numbers of *tweets* from some firms compared to others.

The data was organized by date for each firm before and after it was entered into Diction. The eight alphanumeric identifiers further enabled the researcher to extricate data based on variables such as financial ranking and litigation type. The research questions for this study explored what OIM strategies are used by successful U.S. law firms in social media, and whether there are differences based on annual gross revenue and litigation specialty.

Analysis of data. The researcher used the Statistical Package for Social Sciences (SPSS) program to perform comparative analysis on firm's OIM strategies in Twitter. Repeated measures ANOVA was used to examine the differences in OIM strategies as measured by rhetorical tone of five variables (DV), based on annual gross revenues (IV),litigation specialty type (IV), and the differences over 5 years. The following research questions and hypotheses guided this research study and addressed the stated problem:

R1: Do differences exist in any of the five OIM strategy metrics based on revenues (bottom quartile versus top quartile)?

H_1: At least one of the five OIM strategy metrics will be different based on revenue (bottom quartile versus top quartile).

H_{01}: None of the five OIM strategy metrics will be different based on revenues (bottom quartile versus top quartile).

R2: Do differences exist in any of the five OIM strategy metrics based on specialty (labor law versus intellectual property versus product liability)? H_2:

At least one of the five OIM strategy metrics will be different based on specialty (labor law versus intellectual property versus product liability).

H02: None of the five OIM strategy metrics will be different based on specialty (labor law versus intellectual property versus product liability).

R3: Do differences exist in any of the five OIM strategy metrics based on year (2010 through 2014)?

H3: At least one of the five OIM strategy metrics will be different based on year (2010 through 2014).

H03: None of the five OIM strategy metrics will be different based on year (2010 through 2014).

The independent and dependent variables in this study were continuous. Annual gross revenues were used instead of ordinal financial ranking because they provided a truer picture of the vast differences among firms on the *AmLaw 100* list. The scores of rhetorical tone were also provided as continuous variables in Diction. The Diction z- scores for each firm's rhetorical tone were used as the dependent variables. The scores were normally distributed. The Diction variables have been used in prior OIM studies and are considered to be valid and reliable for the measurement of rhetorical tone in corporate communications. Therefore, the correct statistical test was to use repeated measures ANOVA for a causal comparative analysis of law firms based on annual gross revenues and litigation specialty type

(Gravetter & Wallnau, 2013). The table in Appendix A gives an outline of the instrument and data analysis for each research question.

Ethical Considerations

This study was exempt from Institutional Review Board (IRB) review under the Protection of Human Subjects Act (2009) since the research involved the collection or study of existing data that are publicly available. The researcher conducted a content analysis of social media sites and other publicly available information without violating ethical standards, compromising human subjects, or accessing private company data.

In addition, this analysis did not require a confidentiality disclosure since the data obtained are public information. Although organizational names and financials are included in public industry rankings, the names of law firms used in this study were coded for anonymity. A potential ethical concern is that companies often appear on the same industry lists year after year; thus, a replication of this study may yield a relatively small chance of deducing which firms were sampled. However, social media is publicly available information disseminated by firms themselves, and firms voluntarily disclosed information used in this study. As such, there is no confidentiality breach involved. Since this study used publicly available information, there was not any human research, making the study exempt from IRB review.

Limitations

Some limitations may include issues with regard to use of the list of top revenue-grossing law firms and, therefore, not applicable to the rest of the population. Also, the use of content analysis may pose some problems. One problem is that counting word frequencies or phrases can eliminate meanings of the contexts in which they are written. Certain software applications are designed for specific types of texts, and the choice of dictionary used must be programmed and customizable to the researcher's needs.

Limitations with software. Diction was originally written to analyze tone in political speeches (Hart, 2014; Krippendorff, 2013). Though it has since expanded dictionaries to include all types of corporate communications, its origins remain a concern. It includes customizable dictionaries, along with the ability to select which normative database to use for comparisons. This study used the normative database "corporate business communications" instead of the normative "general" database, which includes scientific and poetic literature, among others (Hart, 2014).

Limitations with content. Though Diction's variables demonstrate OIM in general, with some of its variables tied to the OIM taxonomy in prior studies, it may not have the capability to detect latent meaning in certain types of texts. Legal communications in general are highly regulated, and any conveyance of representation, solicitation, or breach of confidentiality can trigger an ethics violation (Vinson, 2010). Thus, the content on firm's social media sites may not be as directly obvious as it would be for other industries. The analysis of legal web sites and social media could generate problems in accuracy. "Legal explanations emphasize that communicators operate under certain legal conditions; for example, they may have to be licensed or must comply with or avoid violating contractual arrangements" (Krippendorff, 2013, p. 76). Krippendorff (2013) further stated, "Texts obtained in legally regulated contexts reflect the legal constraints under which the institutional communicators who are being studied operate" (p. 76), which could pose a problem in extracting content for placement into the OIM categories.

Limitations of OIM variables. This study was limited to the variables defined by the software used for initial analysis. Diction's categorical variables prove to be the most useful for OIM exploration through rhetorical tone. However, it is limited in scope and other software or types of analysis may yield new or different OIM strategies that go beyond rhetorical measurement.

Limitations of researcher analysis. While the notion that computer searches mask interpretations and meanings was refuted by Krippendorff (2013), some meaning might be lost in the initial analysis via Diction. Large volumes of data can also dilute meaning from individual messages. For example, some blogs or *tweets* may be from a year ago and have a different sentiment than more recent material. Further, the researcher may inadvertently incorrectly categorize content. Finally, mathematical errors could occur if the researcher manipulates data for further analysis. For example, one method of determining whether Diction's scores are statistically significant is to follow Yuthas, Rogers, and Dillard's (2002) method of calculating percentages, which is discussed in Chapter 4.

Summary

The present study used a quantitative methodology with a causal comparative research design, and historical content analysis. Quantitative analysis was needed because the study explored the differences between OIM strategies based on annual gross revenues and litigation specialty. It was an historical analysis since social media communications have been posted and were collected in reverse chronological order until a saturated sample was reached. Further, since OIM is rooted in dramaturgical symbolic interactionist theory, measurement of rhetorical through content analysis was appropriate for this study (Neuendorf, 2002). Diction content analysis software was the tool for analysis. The use of the Diction software was appropriate for this study because of its unique ability to extract rhetorical tone and meaning from otherwise meaningless words and phrases (Krippendorff, 2013).

Moreover, the current study explored the OIM strategies of successful firms via social media in relation to annual gross revenues and litigation specialty. The population selection mirrored prior studies of successful firms (McDonnell & King, 2012). The stratified purposive sample from the *AmLaw 100* firms was chosen based on criteria listed in Chapter 3. The analysis consisted of the most popular social media site among *AmLaw 100* firms, Twitter, in order to provide a deeper understanding of OIM tactics. Twitter was also identified as one of the two most popular social media sites among law firms in general (LexisNexis, 2014b). Data was collected through publicly available organizational postings. Thus, this study did not require confidentiality agreements or agreements for participation. However, law firm names were coded for anonymity.

After social media communications were downloaded and prepared, the researcher used Diction software for textual analysis. Diction has been the categorical instrument in prior OIM studies and has been used along with the Mohamed et al. (1999) OIM taxonomy to identify assertive and defensive themes (Avery & McKay, 2006; Barnes et al., 2013; Chilcutt, 2009; Nagy et al., 2012; O'Keefe & Conway, 2008; Pollach & Kerbler, 2011; Schniederjans et al., 2013; Tyler et al. 2012; Vielhaber & Waltman, 2008). As such, the body of literature supports use of Diction since it has been used and validated in a number of prior OIM studies.

In conclusion, Chapter 4 will commence with data analysis. The sample firm's social media sites were analyzed through Diction software for rhetorical tone on five Master Variables. Chapter 5 will discuss the Diction results and further summarizes the output.

Chapter 4: Data Analysis and Results

Introduction

The purpose of this causal comparative quantitative study was to determine if differences exist in social media OIM strategies based on financial performance and litigation specialty by the largest revenue-grossing U.S. law firms. Exploration of OIM strategies of successful firms via social media is important since gaining public trust is critical for most organizations (Tyler et al., 2012). Given that organizational communications affect perceptions of company image (Pollach & Kerbler, 2011) and social media's popularity continues to grow, this study contributed to OIM research and literature through analysis of OIM strategies in social media. Analysis of law firm's Twitter presence addressed the problem statement: It is not known if there are differences in social media OIM strategies based on financial performance and litigation specialty by the largest revenue-grossing U.S. law firms. Organizations use OIM strategies to gain public trust, achieve status, gain approval among industry constituents, and manage brand image (McDonnell & King, 2013; Saxton & Guo, 2012). Social media as a communication platform can provide great opportunities because of its wide reach and rapid transmission of information. With a larger audience having instantaneous access to information, organizations need to be mindful of their image management efforts.

This study used a quantitative methodology, specifically a causal comparative research design, with an historical content analysis data collection technique. The dependent variables were OIM strategies via social media, measured through rhetorical tone, used by the largest revenue-grossing U.S. law firms. The independent variables were annual gross revenue and litigation specialty type. The study used an historical content analysis to explore law firm's Twitter sites for current and prior organizational posts. The researcher retrieved posts in reverse chronological order until a sufficient number of units was obtained (Krippendorff, 2013). Historical content analysis was performed, similar to prior OIM studies (Barnes et al., 2013; Chilcutt, 2009; Kwok & Yu, 2013; Patelli & Pedrini, 2013; Schniederjans et al., 2013).

The research questions were designed to aid in understanding the OIM strategies used by successful U.S. law firms to manage their brand impressions via social media. The following research question and hypothesis served as a guide to address the stated problem:

R1: Do differences exist in any of the five OIM strategy metrics based on revenues (bottom quartile versus top quartile)?

H_1: At least one of the five OIM strategy metrics will be different based on revenue (bottom quartile versus top quartile).

H_{01}: None of the five OIM strategy metrics will be different based on revenues (bottom quartile versus top quartile).

R2: Do differences exist in any of the five OIM strategy metrics based on specialty (labor law versus intellectual property versus product liability)? H2: At least one of the five OIM strategy metrics will be different based on specialty (labor law versus intellectual property versus product liability).

H02: None of the five OIM strategy metrics will be different based on specialty (labor law versus intellectual property versus product liability).

R3: Do differences exist in any of the five OIM strategy metrics based on year (2010 through 2014)?

H3: At least one of the five OIM strategy metrics will be different based on year (2010 through 2014).

H03: None of the five OIM strategy metrics will be different based on year (2010 through 2014).

The five dependent variables studied were the OIM strategies measured by rhetorical tone of *Optimism, Certainty, Activity, Realism,* and *Commonality* used in social media by the largest revenue-grossing U.S. law firms. The five variables are defined in Appendix C. The independent variables were gross annual revenues and law firm specialty.

Chapter 4 presents a descriptive summary of the population and the sample selection. The industry and population were chosen purposefully to study successful firms strategizing under legal constraints, within an industry facing slowed demand. Understanding OIM strategy used in an industry bound by legal and ethical constraints may aid others in their marketing efforts. This study has particular significance for law firms that face challenges in a very competitive industry. Thus, an exploration of OIM strategy via social media among financially successful law firms may help other firms develop a set of best practices to improve or enhance stakeholder perceptions of company image.

Further, Chapter 4 addresses how data were obtained via organizational social media sites, namely Twitter. Twitter was chosen because it is one of the most popular social media for law firms (LexisNexis, 2014a). Similarly, this study found that Twitter was the most used social media by law firms on the *AmLaw 100* list. Following is a description of the population and sample. This chapter continues with an explanation of how data were collected and examined though Diction text analysis software. The chapter explains the settings adjustments required to run data against the proper normative database. The research questions are answered in their respective order, and descriptive results for each firm are provided.

Descriptive Data

A purposive sample was drawn from the annual *AmLaw 100* list of largest revenue-grossing U.S. law firms. Stratified sampling was used to narrow the sample to six firms to accommodate strata, or subgroups, representative in the population (Krippendorff, 2013). Criteria included having a specialty area, instead of general litigation, to account for the subpopulation of differences in specialty litigation. Further stratification included selecting half the sample firms from the top 25% and bottom 25% of the list for financial objectivity regarding their rankings. Litigation specialty is illustrated in Table 6. The majority of *AmLaw 100* firms listed *general litigation* on their web sites, since these firms typically have multi-state offices and multiple specialties.

Table 6. AmLaw 100 Firms with Designated Specialties using Social Media

Specialty	Total Firms	Blog	Twitter	LinkedIn	Firms fitting criteria
Mergers/acquisitions	7	0	0	0	0
Employment/Labor	7	6	5	5	5
Intellectual Property	12	11	10	10	10
Product Liability	8	6	7	6	6
Bankruptcy	5	2	1	0	0

| Other Specialty | 5 | 5 | 1 | 1 | 0 |
| General Litigation | 66 | Not included in stratified sample. | | | |

Finally, the major criterion for this study was use of Twitter, which was identified as the most popular among the AmLaw 100 list used in this study and law firms in general (LexisNexis, 2014b). Table 7 lists the number of firms using social media sites in descending order of popularity.

Table 7. AmLaw 100 Firms with Social Media

Social Media	Number of firms
Twitter	59
LinkedIn	55
Facebook	42
Google Plus	24
Blogs	13
No social media sites	29

The final sample selection included specialty areas of product liability litigation (PL), intellectual property law (IP), and employment / labor law

(LL). Two firms in each specialty were identified from the top and bottom quartiles of the financial rankings list. For reasons stated in Chapter 2, this study used Twitter for analysis, although firms chosen also showed active social media usage outside of Twitter to better represent the goals of this study. The final sample for this study is shown in Table 8.

Table 8. Criteria for Sample Selection

Specialty Designation	Code	U.S. based	Blogs	Twitter	LinkedIn	Top 25%	Bottom 25%
Employment/Lab or (LL)							
Firm 1	LL1	X	X	X	X	X	
Firm 2	LL2	X	X	X	X		X
Product Liability (PL)							
Firm 1	PL1	X	X	X	X	X	
Firm 2	PL2	X	X	X	X		X

	Intellectual Property (IP)						
Firm 1	IP1	X	X	X	X	X	
Firm 2	IP2	X	X	X	X		X

The final sample consisted of half the firms from the top and bottom quartiles in financial rankings. In other words, this selection represented one firm in each specialty in the top 25% of financial rankings and the second firm in the corresponding specialty from the bottom of the list. The financial differences among the top 25% ranged from $1 billion to $2.2 billion annual gross revenue. The financial range for the bottom 25% was $3.15 million to $3.9 million annual gross revenue. The range of financial rankings among similar-type firms was vastly different. For example, the LL specialty firm at the top earned nearly $1.3 billion, while the LL specialty firm at the bottom earned $3.1 million, a difference of almost $1 billion. The stratification of financial ranking was a worthwhile method to represent the financial variation among firms (Krippendorff, 2013).

Data Analysis Procedures

This causal comparative, quantitative study used rhetorical content analysis for data collection. To interpret the data, the researcher used repeated measures ANOVA for statistical analyses. Descriptive statistics were obtained through text mining to quantify the data in preparation for rhetorical analysis. Law firm's Twitter data were downloaded via specialty browser software, scrubbed, placed into .txt files by the researcher, and run through Diction software. The software condensed data into descriptive categories through such methods as counting word frequencies, occurrences, placements in text, and other quantifiable features of textual data (Neuendorf, 2002; Saldana, 2009). Based on five Master Variables that served as dependent variables in this study, Diction measured the OIM strategies through rhetorical tone in law firm's Twitter posts. It should be noted that this analysis was strictly from an organizational perspective and used only Twitter posts originated by law firms. Prior OIM researchers have relied on content analysis software to analyze rhetorical tone as it relates to OIM theory (Avery & MacKay, 2006; Craig & Brennan, 2012; Craig et al., 2013; Hall et al., 2013; Parhankangas & Ehrlich, 2012; Patelli & Pedrini, 2013; Schniederjans et al., 2013). This study used Diction content analysis software to analyze social media use in a stratified purposive sample of law firms to address the following research questions and hypotheses:

R1: Do differences exist in any of the five OIM strategy metrics based on revenues (bottom quartile versus top quartile)?

H_1: At least one of the five OIM strategy metrics will be different based on revenue (bottom quartile versus top quartile).

H_{01}: None of the five OIM strategy metrics will be different based on revenues (bottom quartile versus top quartile).

R2: Do differences exist in any of the five OIM strategy metrics based on specialty (labor law versus intellectual property versus product liability)? H2: At least one of the five OIM strategy metrics will be different based on specialty (labor law versus intellectual property versus product liability).

H02: None of the five OIM strategy metrics will be different based on specialty (labor law versus intellectual property versus product liability).

R3: Do differences exist in any of the five OIM strategy metrics based on year (2010 through 2014)?

H3: At least one of the five OIM strategy metrics will be different based on year (2010 through 2014).

H03: None of the five OIM strategy metrics will be different based on year (2010 through 2014).

Accordingly, the rhetorical tone variables representing OIM strategies were identified through Diction software. The Statistical Package for Social Sciences (SPSS) software was used to analyze the collected data through descriptive statistics and repeated measures ANOVA for hypothesis testing. The variables studied were the OIM strategies measured by rhetorical tone of *Optimism*, *Certainty*, *Activity*, *Realism*, and *Commonality* (dependent variables) used in social media by the largest revenue-grossing U.S. law firms. The variables are defined in Appendix C. The independent variables were gross annual revenues and litigation specialty type. Data were downloaded from Twitter, run through Diction software, exported to

Microsoft Excel spreadsheets, and then exported into SPSS for further statistical analysis.

The first step was to verify that all data were normally distributed, as a requirement for correlational analysis. The second step was to analyze all variables to determine direction and strength of correlations of the five dependent variables to financial ranking and litigation specialty. The third step involved analysis of differences in rhetorical tone across the 5 years studied. Lastly, the researcher analyzed the data against Diction's normative scores.

Preparation of data. In total, 160,005 words were analyzed for this study from over 9,885 tweets originated by law firms and collected from organizational sites. Twitter data were downloaded into spreadsheet format, and files were then converted into text (.txt) format. In preparation for Diction analysis, batches of *tweets* for each firm over a period of 5 years were assigned eight identifiers: (1) social media site and year posted; (2) law firm specialty type, two firms in each specialty (IP, LL, or PL); (3) Firm 1 of each specialty type from the upper quartile or Firm 2 of each specialty type from the lower quartile; (4) initials (undisclosed for anonymity) of law firm; (5) posting ending dates; (6) posting starting dates; (7) number of posts; and (8) financial ranking on *AmLaw 100* list. To maintain firm anonymity, a unique eight-character alphanumeric identifier was assigned to each text uploaded to Diction. In this way, each text could be linked to Twitter and year posted, while maintaining the financial ranking and specialty of each firm. For example, TW LL 2 XY 314 912 2100 98 would represent a fictional firm on Twitter (TW), specializing in labor law (LL), positioned as the second firm (2) in the lower quartile, with firm initials XY, with tweets from March 2014 going back to September 2012, having 2,100 total posts, and ranking number 98 on the *AmLaw 100* list.

Rhetorical tone analysis through Diction. Diction 7.0 software (Hart, 2014) was used because of its ability to apply descriptive and thematic content analysis to text. It provides a "scientific method for determining the tone of a verbal message" through use of a built-in database utilizing 50,000 previously analyzed texts (Hart, 2014). Diction contains over 31 dictionaries and categorizes text under five Master Variables and a myriad of sub-variables (Patelli & Pedrini, 2013). Researchers can use general norms or select from among 36 sub-categories (e.g., speeches, poetry, newspaper editorials, business reports, etc.) to gain a comparative assessment. The output consists of numeric files for later statistical analysis.

Diction searches text for the following five Master Variables:

☐*Certainty*: Language indicating resoluteness, inflexibility, and completeness and a tendency to speak *ex cathedra*.

☐   *Activity*: Language featuring movement, change, implementation of ideas, and avoidance of inertia.

☐ *Optimism*: Language endorsing some person, group, concept, or event or highlighting their positive entailments.

☐ *Realism*: Language describing tangible, immediate, recognizable matters that affect people's everyday lives.

☐ *Commonality*: Language highlighting the agreed-upon values of a group and rejecting idiosyncratic modes of engagement (Hart, 2014).

The Master Variables have been converted to z-scores and standardized through a process of addition and subtraction of sub-variables. Researchers may create their own formulas with sub-variables, as has been done in prior studies. However, the Master Variables cannot be reformulated. Therefore, Diction output can be directly compared to other studies using Diction's variables. As a result, the researcher was able to obtain standardized scores, frequencies, percentages, and other quantifiable features, such as "insistence" words that appeared frequently in content. Lastly, Diction settings were adjusted to account for differences between long and short passages, as was the case with 140-character *tweets*, as opposed to lengthier postings found in blogs and other social media (Hart, 2014). Settings were also adjusted to compare documents from Business Corporate Public Relations (BCPR) communications, rather than the General normative setting default, to ensure that social media content was not compared to text from poetry, sciences, and other irrelevant content.

To test these settings, the researcher conducted a pilot study with sample texts from each of the six firms to compare output from the General norm setting to the BCPR norm setting. The latter setting was found to be more appropriate for analysis of social media. Diction categorized the data into the five Master Variable categories, and the results were presented in numerical form in comparison to Diction's range of normative scores for each category. Diction output "flagged" the variables that were out of the normative range and presented the numerical results of 35 sub-variables, in addition to the five Master Variables. The results of this trial are presented later in this section.

Analysis of Diction scores. Diction output for each firm's *tweets* was exported to spreadsheet software Excel for further analysis. Exporting the data enabled the researcher to manually analyze the data. Although Diction "flagged" the outliers in each category, some were only slightly more than 1 standard deviation of the mean, while other variables had a visibly large difference. For the sake of objectivity, the researcher calculated the percentage difference of Diction scores per firm against the norm generated by Diction's BCPR categories. This calculation was completed in accordance with prior literature by using a 2% difference on the Master Variables as a statistically significant difference (Yuthas et al., 2002). The same method was also used by Patelli and Pedrini (2013) in their OIM study using Diction software.

The researcher examined the percentage differences from the variable's respective means. Prior OIM researchers using Diction formulated a process to check for statistically significant differences beyond what Diction output indicates (Patelli & Pedrini, 2013). Statistically significant levels of 2% for Master Variables and 20% for sub-variables were taken from Yuthas et al. (2002). For example, the difference is considered significant when the value of the Master Variable *Optimism* deviates at least 2% from the Diction normative value. The *Optimism* category in Diction is obtained from the following combination of sub-variables: *Praise, Satisfaction, Inspiration*, MINUS *Blame, Hardship* and *Denial*. Its value tends to vary less than the values of the sub- variables. Therefore, the significance level for Master Variables is set to be lower than that of sub-variables. Variances of at least 2% are considered to be statistically significant (Patelli & Pedrini, 2013).

Diction software exemplifies the rhetorical tone of messages that are representative of OIM (Schniederjans et al., 2013). Diction's five Master Variables demonstrate sentiments of *Certainty* (i.e., resoluteness, inflexibility, completeness, and honesty), *Optimism* (i.e., accomplishments, endorsements, or positive verbiage), *Activity* (i.e., movement, change, and innovations), *Realism* (i.e., tangible, current, and immediate matters), and *Commonality* (i.e., emphasis on group values; Hart, 2014). According to prior literature, the five Master Variables are representative of OIM strategies and reflect an organization's attempts to project itself to the public (Avery & McKay, 2006; Craig & Brennan, 2012; Craig et al., 2013; Hall et al., 2013;

Parhankangas & Ehrlich, 2012;Patelli & Pedrini, 2013; Schniederjans et al., 2013). The analysis of OIM strategies is addressed in Chapter 5.

Statistical analysis. Data from Excel were transferred to SPSS for statistical analysis. The researcher obtained descriptive statistics for each of the variables and performed a normalcy check to ensure the data were normally distributed. This study was set at a 95% confidence interval. Each of the five dependent variables satisfied skewness and kurtosis requirements for normality. The Shapiro-Wilks test for dependent and independent variables showed normal distribution. The probability of sphericity using Mauchly's test was less than or equal to alpha .05. Therefore, the assumption of sphericity was met. The researcher next used repeated measures ANOVA to answer Research Questions 1, 2, and 3.

Validity and reliability. Diction 7.0 is a Windows-based content analysis program that uses five dictionaries based on five Master Variables (Hart, 2014). Diction software has been used with success in prior OIM studies and has been validated through its measurement of OIM tactics in both quantitative and qualitative studies (Bravo et al.,2012; Craig & Brennan, 2012; Craig et al., 2013; Hall et al., 2012; Parhankangas & Ehrlich, 2012; Patelli & Pedrini, 2013; Tyler et al., 2012). The body of literature supports the use of Diction for OIM analysis of various corporate communications (Bravo et al., 2012; Craig & Brennan, 2012; Craig et al., 2013; Hall et al.,

2012; Parhankangas &Ehrlich, 2012; Patelli & Pedrini, 2013; Tyler et al., 2012).

Further, through use of Diction's built-in dictionaries, researchers can control for problems such as inter-rater reliability issues, inconsistencies, and subjectivity. The dictionaries are based on a vast array of narratives yielding both empirical and measurement validity (Patelli & Pedrini, 2013). Use of Diction provides stability in analysis, and its availability and use by others makes it highly replicable (Krippendorff, 2013). In addition, Diction's variables have been converted to z-scores and present the user with a range of scores +/- 1 standard deviation from the mean. Unlike raw scores, z- scores enable direct comparison of studies using Diction for analysis (Hart, 2014). Thus, per the literature, Diction is a valid, reliable, and consistent tool for measurement of rhetorical tone. As indicated in Chapter 2, rhetorical tone has been tied to OIM strategy. Thus, the five rhetorical tone categories in Diction were used to address the research questions for this study.

Pilot study. The researcher conducted a pilot study to test the validity of Diction scores through manual analysis of a select number of *tweets*. First, the researcher conducted a trial analysis of *tweets*, followed by a trial analysis of organizational blogs, to determine which of Diction's settings needed modification. The researcher used the standard dictionary first to see how the text from social media postings compared to the General database. The General database gave results compared to the total normative database of 40 scores based on a 50,000-item sample of discourse and 36 sub-categories, including speeches, poetry, newspaper editorials, business reports, scientific documents, television scripts, and telephone conversations. All texts were produced in the United States between 1945 and the present. The default setting in Diction is All: All Cases (Hart, 2014). Diction's output gave the score alongside a range of normative scores for comparison. The "high" and "low" scores represented +1 standard deviation (s.d.) and -1 s.d. from the mean, respectively.

Further, for longer selections, such as blogs, the settings had to be modified; however, settings did not have to be adjusted to answer the research questions since *tweets* are limited to 140 characters. The researcher treated the settings with the Averaged option (i.e., the default setting), which generated one set of scores for the entire passage, regardless of length. Though Diction can accommodate passages up to 500,000 words, Averaged is the preferred setting for large numbers of texts of varying size. Shorter selections were treated through the Report Extrapolations setting, the default option, which corrected for small file sizes by standardization to a 500-word basis (Hart, 2014).

It should be noted that Diction makes statistical accommodations for homographs (i.e., words spelled the same but having different meanings). The word *lead* for example, can denote (1) qualities of command or (2) a metal found in nature. Roughly 10% of Diction's 10,000 search words are homographs. *Confounding homographs* are terms denoting dissimilar ideas or objects. Diction deals with such terms by applying different weights to a word's various meanings. For example, research shows that the word *saw* serves as the past tense of *see* 67% of the time and as a carpenter's implement 33% of the time. Thus, if *saw* were to occur 10 times in a text, it would be given a rating of 6.7 in a Bodily Processes dictionary and a value of 3.3 in a Household Tools dictionary. All such calculations were extrapolated from statistical counts provided in Easton's edited handbook *Word Frequency Dictionary* (as cited in Hart, 2014).

Second, the researcher changed the General normative database to the BCPR normative database for further analysis of social media. Each text was run against the default General normative database first to see if the results were different for the law firms in the sample. The researcher chose BCPR as the normative base (n = 163). According to Diction's manual, this category is a broad-based collection of official mission statements, public pronouncements, and C.E.O. speeches in behalf of major American corporations from the 1960s through the present. Includes manufacturing companies (e.g., Boise-Cascade), mining and construction (e.g., Flour Daniel), transportation and telecommunications (e.g., A.T.&T.), as well as, financial and service-based industries (e.g., Federated Department stores, H&R Block, etc.). (Hart, 2014, p.45)

Based on the trial analysis, Diction's BCPR normative database was used rather than the General database.

This section provides the sample results for a comparison of Diction scores between the BCPR and General databases. The raw scores were examined first to assess whether scores fell outside Diction's normative range. Next, the researcher analyzed Diction scores in Excel to see how they related to statistical interpretations in the literature. Then, the researcher conducted statistical analysis via repeated measures ANOVA in the order of the corresponding research questions.

The sample analysis against the general normative range (GNR) for sample data showed that all six firms scored low on the Master Variables, *Realism* (firm's range was low 38.08-42.27; GNR was 46.1-52.62) and *Certainty* (firm's range was low 38.54-45.15; GNR was 46.9-51.96). In addition, all six firms scored extremely high, between 39.28 and 46.32 (GNR was .3-15.04), on *Numerical Terms* and extremely low on *Familiarity*. The other variables either had slight differences outside the standard range provided by Diction or did not provide conclusive information.

In addition, the scores from each firm's Twitter account were compared to the BCPR normative database. The scores reported were fractionated with some integers less than 1 due to the statistical corrections in Diction. The results are reported against the normative range of scores, which represent +1 s.d. and -1 s.d. from the mean. The means are derived from prior analysis of 50,000 texts drawn from a wide variety of sectors and English language documents since the early 1960s. Calculations for Master Variables are explained in the Diction manual (Hart, 2014).

In summary, the results showed that the General normative database was not able to detect the nuances of specifically designed databases for public relations material. Therefore, the researcher chose to run the analysis with the BCPR normative settings to present a truer comparison of texts. A sample of the range differences between the two normative settings is shown in Table 9.

Table 9. Comparison of Normative Range for Diction Master Variables

Master Variables	Activity	Optimism	Certainty	Realism	Commonality
General Normative Database	46.74-55.48	6.37-52.25	6.9-51.96	46.1-52.62	46.86-52.28
Business Corporate Public Relations	48.16-52.43	48.21-55.58	48..43-52.71	4.44-50.66	48.4-54.08

| Normative |
| Database |

Results of Diction scores. Diction scores for each firm were exported to Excel spreadsheet software for comparison of variables collectively over the 5 years reviewed. Doing so provided an overview of each firm's rhetorical tone and a base for answering the research questions. The researcher examined Master Variable scores that varied at least 2% from Diction normative scores. According to prior research, Master Variable scores varying 2% and sub-variable scores deviating more than 20% were considered statistically significant (Patelli & Pedrini, 2013; Yuthas et al., 2002).

The researcher analyzed close to 10,000 tweets for all firms, dating from February

2009 to March 2014. The tweets analyzed were originated by the six law firms in the sample and used to measure the OIM messages strategically placed for public view on Twitter. Output is presented in Table 10.

Table 10. Collective Twitter Results Master Variables

Firm	Activity	Optimism	Certainty	Realism	Commonality
LL1	50.31	48.92	39.9*	44.35*	48.91

LL2	52.36	50.26	45.21*	41.78*	47.88*
IP1	49.63	50.26	41.9*	43.01*	50.41
IP2	49.89	49.01	37.91*	41.48*	50.27
PL1	49.55	51.85	39.96*	41.94*	50.06
PL2	47.52*	43.95*	40.56*	45.09*	49.12

*Lower than Diction's normative range

**Higher than Diction's normative range

The Diction scores in Table 10 show the outlier variables either above or below Diction's BCPR normative range, providing a quick overview of rhetorical tone of the sample law firm's Twitter posts. Overall, the firms as a group exhibited the following characteristics on the five Master Variables:

Activity. Only firm PL2 scored low in this variable; the rest were within the normative range. As a group, the average score was low, at -1% below the average normative mean. Following Yuthas et al. (2002), this was not a statistically significant difference from the Diction normative range for this variable.

Optimism. Only firm PL2 scored low in this variable; the rest were within the normative range. As with *Activity*, the average group score was low. The average of all firms was -5% below the average normative mean, which was more than the 2% difference set by prior researchers (Patelli & Pedrini, 2013; Yuthas et al., 2002). Therefore, law firms had statistically significant lower *Optimism* than the Diction normative average.

Certainty. All firms scored low, between 37.91 and 45.21 (BCPR 48.43-52.71). The variation of average scores from the mean average normative scores was 19% lower. Therefore, the law firms exhibited lower *Certainty* than was expected for BCPR.

Realism. Five firms scored low (between 41.48 and 44.35), while firm PL2 scored 45.09 within range (BCPR 44.4-50.66). As a whole, the average variation of scores from the normative range was lower than Diction's BPCR range. According to prior studies using Diction, this was a statistically significant finding.

Commonality. Firm LL2 was the only firm that scored low on *Commonality*. However, the average score for the group was lower than the mean average normative score overall by 4%. Therefore, there was a statistically significant difference according to Yuthas et al. (2002).

Although the former were results for the Master Variables, Diction flagged several sub-variables as outliers. The following outlines firm's Diction scores on select sub-variables in preparation for further statistical analysis and to compare Diction scores to prior studies in Chapter 5. Collectively, the sub-variables *Accomplishment, Ambivalence, Familiarity, Tenacity, Praise, Present Concern,* and *Leveling Terms* showed lower overall scores for all Twitter data for all firms than Diction's normative average. The collective analysis was done to provide a basis for subsequent analysis in breaking down Twitter data to answer the research questions.

Twitter analysis as a group. All six firms had a statistically significant high *Numeric Terms* variable with an average score of 43.99, which was 357% higher than the 9.63 normative range average. As a group, these law firms scored low on *Familiarity* (-49%), *Realism* (-10%), *Certainty* (-19%),

Ambivalence (-60%), *Tenacity* (-70%), *Leveling Terms* (-80%), *Hardship* (-7%), *Human Interest* (-76%), *Centrality* (-54%), and *Optimism* (-5%). Collectively, they scored high on *Variety* (7%). *Blame* was 1% higher for the group than the normative mean, due to PL2's high score. Firm PL2 was the only firm that scored within the range on *Realism* (45.09) and scored the highest in *Human Interest* (19.89), although this was still within the normative range (between 14.27 and 44.85).

Twitter analysis single firms. Firm PL2 was different in other categories as well. Although within range and, therefore, not a statistically significant deviation, it scored well above the other firms on *Ambivalence, Tenacity, Leveling Terms, Human Interest*, and *Variety*. Firm PL2 scored much higher than the others, with a statistically significant difference of 333% on *Blame* (Diction score 5.59 with a mean of 1.29) and 136% on *Hardship* (score 10.16 with a mean of 4.31). Firm PL2 scored highest on *Aggression* compared to other firms, although still within the normative range. Firm PL2 was also below the range on *Centrality* and scored well below the other firms at 0.19 with a -97% difference from the mean of 6.59. It scored the lowest on *Optimism* (Diction score 43.95, the only firm outside of the normative range, mean 51.9) with a difference of -15%. Other differences among single firms were the following: Firm PL1 was the lowest on *Hardship*, falling below the mean range with a Diction score of 0.6 at an -86% difference from the mean. Firm LL1 scored the highest in *Cooperation* at 13.22, a 123% difference. Firm LL2 had an extremely high *Insistence* score of 242.62 for a 345%

difference from the mean normative average. IP1 scored the highest on *Concreteness* at 102% and *Past Concern* at 204% of the normative average mean. Firm IP2 scored the highest in *Communication* with a 108% difference.

The Diction scores and their significance to OIM research are deliberated in Chapter 5. To meet the goals of this study, it was necessary to conduct further analysis of the scores in terms of revenue category, litigation specialty type, and variation over a 5-

year period. The research questions were subsequently answered by exporting the Diction scores from Excel into SPSS. Descriptive statistics were obtained for the dependent variables, which are presented in Table 11.

Table 11. Distribution of Dependent Variables

	N	Minimu	Maximu	Mean	Std.
Activity	6	47.52	52.36	49.8767	1.55
Optimism	6	43.95	51.85	49.0417	2.71
Certainty	6	37.91	45.21	40.9067	2.47
Realism	6	41.48	45.09	42.9417	1.48
Commonality	6	47.88	50.41	49.4417	.982
ValidN	6				
(listwise)					

The independent variable, annual gross revenues, was analyzed next. Descriptive statistics of the data revealed that the minimum was $315,000,000 and the maximum was 1,076,000,000 for the sample's annual gross revenues. The mean was $669,750,000 with a standard deviation of 365,557,348. The independent variable, litigation specialty type, was represented equally across six firms specializing in labor law, intellectual property law, or product liability law.

The researcher performed a normalcy test to assure the data were approximately normally distributed. Although it is necessary to report measures and standard errors of the normalcy test, data need to only be approximately normally distributed. Tests of skewness and kurtosis were conducted using a Shapiro-Wilks test. The results of the Shapiro-Wilks test revealed the independent variable revenue and the five dependent variables were above $p > .05$ and, therefore, normally distributed.

The Shapiro-Wilks test ($p > .05$) showed that the data for independent variable annual revenue were approximately normally distributed, with a skewness of 0.066 ($SE = 0.845$) and kurtosis of -3.049 ($SE = 1.741$). Division of skewness and kurtosis measures by their corresponding standard error (SE) yielded z-scores of .078 and -1.751, respectively. Both numbers fell between -1.96 and 1.96 and, therefore, within the normalcy range.

Similarly, the researcher conducted tests for normalcy, kurtosis, and skewness on the dependent variables. The significance level for each variable using the Shapiro-Wilks test was above $p > .05$. The skewness measure divided by its SE also suggested a normal distribution for each of the five dependent variables. Division of skewness and kurtosis measures by their corresponding SE resulted in z-scores of .213 and -1.160 for *Activity*; 1.887 and 1.894 for *Optimism*; 1.221 and 1.013 for *Certainty*; 0.753 and 0.924 for *Realism*; and 0.852 and 0.345 for *Commonality*.

Further visual inspections of Q-Q plots and box plots showed normal distributions. In addition, the researcher conducted a Pearson correlation to determine if any of the dependent variables were correlated. Although no significant correlations were found among the dependent variables in the Twitter data used for this study, it is interesting to note the trial blog data found a positive correlation between *Certainty* and *Realism* ($p < .05$, two-tailed).

The researcher exported 30 Diction scores for each dependent variable, representative of six firms over a 5-year period, into Excel for descriptive analysis. The data were subsequently run through SPSS using repeated measures ANOVA using a .05 level of significance. Repeated measures ANOVA was the most appropriate method for answering the research questions central to this study. Results corresponding to research question one are presented below. Comparison of scores between upper and lower-revenue quartiles are listed in Table 12, along with the *SE*, *p* value, and corresponding *F* ratio on within-groups variance.

R1: Do differences exist in any of the five OIM strategy metrics based on revenues (bottom quartile versus top quartile)?

H1: At least one of the five OIM strategy metrics will be different based on revenue (bottom quartile versus top quartile).

H01: None of the five OIM strategy metrics will be different based on revenues (bottom quartile versus top quartile).

Table 12. Comparison of Rhetorical Tone Between Upper and Lower-revenue Quartiles

OIM Metric	Revenue	*M*	*SE*	*F*	*p*
Optimism	Low	48.02	1.19	1.86	.25
	High	50.32	1.19		
Certainty	Low	38.19	0.84	6.55	.06
	High	41.23	0.84		
Activity	Low	49.47	0.40	0.20	.68
	High	49.22	0.40		
Realism	High	41.38	1.11	2.23	.21
	Low	48.12	5.22		
Commonality	High	49.04	5.22	1.54	.28
	Low	49.04	5.22		

The higher revenue firms scored consistently higher in *Optimism* each year, although the scores were within Diction's normative range. The low revenue firms scored lower in *Optimism* compared to Diction's normative range. While all five firms scored lower on *Certainty* than Diction's normative range in each year, the higher revenue firms tended to exhibit higher levels of *Certainty*. This was not quite significant at $p = .06$ but was close enough to merit further consideration. The variable *Activity* showed no deviation from Diction's normative range, and there was no significant difference between high- and low-revenue firms. The fourth dependent variable, *Realism*, showed that all firms were below Diction's normative range. The mean for all scores was 42.55 with $SE = 0.79$. There was no statistically significant difference among higher and lower- revenue firms. The last dependent variable, *Commonality*, did not show significant differences based on revenue group; however, lower-revenue firms scored lower than Diction's normative range. In total, 12 of the 30 *Commonality* scores were below the lowest range given in Diction.

Although the sub-variables were not central to this study, it is interesting to note differences between the revenue groups. In the trial collective analysis, firms in the top 25% of the financial rankings were compared to those in the bottom 25% of the list. Firms in the high revenue category scored lower on *Ambivalence*, *Blame*, and *Present Concern* and higher on *Collectives*, *Cooperation*, and *Concreteness*.

Next, the researcher performed an analysis to identify differences in OIM strategy, as measured by rhetorical tone, among firms specializing in different litigation types. Repeated measures ANOVA was used to answer research question two:

R2: Do differences exist in any of the five OIM strategy metrics based on specialty (labor law versus intellectual property versus product liability)? H2: At least one of the five OIM strategy metrics will be different based on specialty (labor law versus intellectual property versus product liability).

H02: None of the five OIM strategy metrics will be different based on specialty (labor law versus intellectual property versus product liability).

Differences by law firm specialty in mean scores, *SE*, *F*, and *p* values are listed in Table 13. The analysis found no statistically significant difference in rhetorical tone based on litigation specialty type among law firms used in this study. As such, the five metrics used to measure OIM strategies are not different based on specialty type.

Table 13. Differences in Rhetorical Tone Among Specialty

OIM Metric	Specialty	M	SE	F	p
Optimism	LL	49.22	1.52	1.20	.42
	IP	50.81	1.52		
	PL	47.49	1.52		
Certainty	LL	40.23	1.80	0.22	.82
	IP	40.16	1.80		
	PL	38.75	1.80		
Activity	LL	49.90	0.34	2.76	.21
	IP	49.38	0.34		
	PL	49.76	0.34		
Realism	LL	43.09	1.91	0.08	.92
	IP	42.00	1.91		
	PL	42.56	1.91		
Commonality	LL	47.82	0.67	1.05	.45
	IP	49.15	0.67		
	PL	48.77	0.6		

However, product liability firms scored lower than the Diction normative range on the *Optimism* variable. While *Certainty* scores did not show a significant difference among specialty types, all firm categories were lower than Diction's normative range. The *Activity* variable showed that all six firms were within the normative range. *Realism*, on the other hand, reflected low firm means throughout, without showing a significant difference among specialty types. Lastly, labor law firms were the only group scoring lower than Diction's normative range on the dependent variable *Commonality*.

While Diction's sub-variables were not a principal concern in this study, the researcher noted differences among sub-variables based on litigation specialty. In a collaborative Twitter analysis by specialty type, labor law firms showed low *Ambivalence*, *Tenacity*, and *Praise* values, in addition to having among the lowest scores in *Human Interest*, *Present Concern*, and *Rapport*. They were also the highest in *Exclusion*, well above the range. The product liability firms were the lowest in *Spatial Terms*, although they were within the normative range and were also low in *Accomplishment*, *Centrality*, and *Rapport*. The intellectual property firms scored low in *Accomplishment*, *Tenacity*, *Leveling Terms*, and *Human Interest*.

The final research question was answered through repeated measures ANOVA to measure differences based on 5 years of Twitter data for each of the six firms. The *tweets* for each firm were separated into years from 2010 to 2014 for a 5-year analysis of rhetorical tone based on the five dependent variables. Research question three and associated hypothesis are reflected below:

R3: Do differences exist in any of the five OIM strategy metrics based on year (2010 through 2014)?

H3: At least one of the five OIM strategy metrics will be different based on year (2010 through 2014).

H03: None of the five OIM strategy metrics will be different based on year (2010 through 2014).

An overall comparison of rhetorical tone over 5 years is provided in Table 14. The comparison is based on the five OIM variables averaged over a 5-year period for all firms. In general, all firms over 5 years were within Diction's normative range for variables *Optimism* and *Activity*. All firms over 5 years were lower than Diction's normative range in *Certainty* and *Realism*, and all firms scored lower than the Diction normative range in *Commonality* in 2010 and 2012.

Table 14. Comparison of Rhetorical Tone Over 5 Years

OIM Metric	Year	M	SE	F	p
Optimism	2010	49.41	1.55	0.70	.60
	2011	48.36	1.46		
	2012	49.94	0.39		
	2013	49.28	0.46		
	2014	48.87	1.13		

Certainty	2010	39.19	1.88	2.07	.12
	2011	42.36	0.97		
	2012	41.21	0.89		
	2013	38.21	1.64		
	2014	37.59	1.91		
Activity	2010	49.66	0.40	3.67	.02
	2011	51.34	0.30		
	2012	49.03	0.67		
	2013	48.27	1.05		
	2014	48.44	0.42		
Realism	2010	39.89	2.04	3.09	.04
	2011	40.05	2.10		
	2012	44.38	0.94		
	2013	43.99	0.87		
	2014	44.43	0.92		
Commonality	2010	48.39	0.58	0.46	.77
	2011	49.17	0.46		
	2012	48.31	0.87		
	2013	48.58	0.58		
	2014	48.47	0.38		

Analysis through repeated measures ANOVA suggested variables *Optimism*, *Certainty*, and *Commonality* did not show a statistically significant difference over a 5- year period. Mauchly's test revealed that sphericity was not a problem for any of the variables. However, OIM measures based on *Activity* and *Realism* showed some significant differences for firms over a 5-year period. Significant differences existed between Year 5 (2014) and Year 2 (2011) among the five firms for the variable *Activity*. Although the threshold of significance is $p = .05$, years one (2010) and five (2014) showed nearly significant differences in *Activity* ($p = .058$). A Bonferroni post hoc test was conducted by the researcher to determine whether this assumption held true. Post hoc tests are used when a test shows initial significance. The Bonferroni test takes into account errors in multiple tests, giving an adjustment pairwise.

The Bonferroni test confirmed the differences in rhetorical tone among the five firms between years 2010 and 2014 for the variable *Activity* ($p = .04$).

The dependent variable *Realism* also suggested differences in rhetorical tone between years. The statistical analysis using repeated measures ANOVA showed significant differences in *Realism* based on years $p = .039$. However, the Bonferroni post hoc test showed no significant differences for all firms on any of the variables over a 5-year period.

Summary

Nearly 10,000 *tweets* originating from law firms were analyzed in the present study. Thirty batches of data were run through Diction software for six law firms for each of 5 years, amounting to over 160,000 words. The dependent variables were OIM strategies measured in rhetorical tone through Diction content analysis software, as used in prior OIM studies outlined in the literature review. The independent variables were annual gross revenues, delineated as high- and low-revenue firms based on upper and lower quartile rankings of the *AmLaw 100* list. This chapter discussed the findings in terms of firm's rhetorical tone in relation to Diction software's normative range for BCPR. Scores above and below the normative range are interpreted in Chapter 5.

In addition, the researcher analyzed the content of organizational *tweets* to compare similarities and differences among law firms in upper and lower quartiles of the *AmLaw 100* list to answer the first research question: Do differences exist in any of the five OIM strategy metrics based on revenue (bottom quartile versus top quartile)? The results indicated that lower-revenue firms scored lower on *Optimism* than did higher revenue firms and were lower than the Diction normative range. All firms scored lower than the Diction normative range on variables *Certainty* and *Realism*. All six firms scored within the normal range in *Activity*. The lower-income firms scored lower than the normative range on the variable *Commonality*. Although none of the variables showed a statistically significant difference between high- and low-revenue firms, the variable *Certainty* was almost statistically significant at $p = .06$.

Accordingly, the second research question in the present study addressed firm similarities or differences in rhetorical tone based on litigation specialty type: *Do differences exist in any of the five OIM strategy metrics based on specialty (labor law versus intellectual property versus product liability)?* The results confirmed that the product liability firms scored consistently lower on *Optimism, Certainty*, and *Realism* than the other litigation types. Although all firm types scored lower than the Diction normative scores on *Certainty* and *Realism*, no significant differences existed among the three litigation specialty types. The labor law firms were lower than other firm types in *Commonality* and lower than the Diction normative scores.

The last research question examined differences in firm's rhetorical tone over a 5- year period: *Do differences exist in any of the five OIM strategy metrics based on year (2010 through 2014)?* The study found that all six firms scored lower than the Diction normative range for the 5-year period on *Certainty* and *Realism*. The *Activity* scores over the same 5-year period were within range for all six firms. However, there was a statistically significant difference between Year 2 (2011) and Year 5 (2014). There was also a difference between Year 1 (2010) and Year 5 (2014), although not statistically significant at $p = .058$. In addition, the *Commonality* scores were lower in 2010 and 2012 than the Diction normative range overall.

A discussion of these findings is presented in Chapter 5. Some firms had individual outliers on certain variables, while others showed patterns within certain litigation specialties. Further, other sub-variables were prevalent within firms of the upper quartile versus the lower quartile in financial rankings. In addition, there were some notable differences among firms in their Twitter postings. Firm PL2 continued to show significant differences from other firms, as well as from its own specialty group. Chapter 5 provides a discussion of how the Diction variables relate to the OIM tactics used by law firms and explores how they relate to the OIM taxonomy presented in the literature review. The chapter examines the reasons for differences, if any, in OIM metrics among firms based on revenue, litigation specialty, and 5-year time period.

Consequently, Chapter 5 includes the conclusions reached in this study and the ways they may be applied to law firms. Since financially successful firm's practices are often benchmarked in other industries (McDonnell & King, 2013), Chapter 5 addresses whether the results are applicable to other organizations. Finally, the researcher discusses limitations of the current study and areas for further examination, along with theoretical and practical implications of the findings. The chapter concludes with recommendations for future research and practice based on the results of this study.

Chapter 5: Summary, Conclusions, and Recommendations

Introduction

The purpose of this quantitative, causal comparative study was to determine if differences existed in social media OIM strategies based on financial performance and litigation specialty of the largest revenue-grossing U.S. law firms. This study was conducted to understand OIM use via social media by successful firms, which are often identified through their appearance on coveted industry lists (McDonnell & King, 2013). Consequently, the goal of many organizations is to attain approval, status, and prestige among various stakeholders (Highhouse et al., 2009), and many attempt to do so by using OIM in their corporate communications. Organizational impression management involves controlling information in order to influence stakeholder's perceptions about an organization.

Social media has become an important communication vehicle for organizations of all types. Social media's popularity, mass communication capabilities, and rapid dissemination of information differentiate it from traditional communications. As a result, this research on the use of social media as a communications platform is a timely and relevant contribution to OIM literature due to the growing popularity of social media and its rapid adoption among organizations. Further, this study intended to discover how

OIM is used in an industry constrained by legal and ethical boundaries, to the point that many law firms refuse to engage (Vinson, 2010).

This study showed that use of the social media site Twitter among the largest U.S. law firms is relatively prevalent (LexisNexis, 2014b) and can be used to organizational advantage. Using a causal comparative design to examine social media communications initiated by a stratified purposive sample of law firms, textual, rhetorical content analysis was used to extract OIM strategies from social media. Taken together, OIM via social media has important implications for organizations that wish to utilize it to their advantage. Specifically, others in the legal industry may benefit from knowledge about how the top grossing U.S. law firms use OIM via social media.

Chapter 5 begins with an overview of the reasons the study was conducted and the findings as they relate to OIM strategies. Chapter 5 discusses the results and implications as they correspond to the research questions through examination of differences among high- and low-revenue firms, litigation specialty type, over a 5-year period. The results are compared to prior OIM research findings. Finally, Chapter 5 presents a discussion of theoretical and practical implications of the findings, limitations of the study, and future implications, with recommendations for further research.

Summary of the Study

Social media's power to influence public opinion of consumers and other stakeholders regarding organizational image cannot be understated (Brennan et al., 2013). This study has added to the general body of research on OIM through examination of strategies used in Twitter as the organizational communication tool. Specifically, this study may assist law firms in carefully positioning their image in social media to effectively communicate a desired identity and manage external impressions.

The researcher began by downloading social media postings initiated by law firms from March 2014 and proceeding in reverse chronological order until the researcher obtained a sufficient number of units for analysis over a 5-year period. Textual and rhetorical content analysis was applied to content on firm's social media sites. The study used a quantitative methodology, a causal comparative research design, with an historical content analysis data collection technique. The textual analysis tool was Diction 7.0 software, which extracted rhetorical tone and provided a descriptive summary of variables linked to OIM strategy in prior studies. The researcher further examined the strength of these variables against the Diction normative database through Yuthas et al.'s (2002) method of statistical significance. Finally, the researcher conducted repeated measures ANOVA to answer the following research questions and hypotheses that guided this study:

R1: Do differences exist in any of the five OIM strategy metrics based on revenues (bottom quartile versus top quartile)?

H1: At least one of the five OIM strategy metrics will be different based on revenue (bottom quartile versus top quartile).

H01: None of the five OIM strategy metrics will be different based on revenues (bottom quartile versus top quartile).

R2: Do differences exist in any of the five OIM strategy metrics based on specialty (labor law versus intellectual property versus product liability)? H2: At least one of the five OIM strategy metrics will be different based on specialty (labor law versus intellectual property versus product liability).

H02: None of the five OIM strategy metrics will be different based on specialty (labor law versus intellectual property versus product liability).

R3: Do differences exist in any of the five OIM strategy metrics based on year (2010 through 2014)?

H3: At least one of the five OIM strategy metrics will be different based on year (2010 through 2014).

H03: None of the five OIM strategy metrics will be different based on year (2010 through 2014).

The independent variables were gross annual revenues, delineated as upper and lower quartiles of the *AmLaw 100* list, and litigation specialty type. The dependent variables were the OIM strategies measured by rhetorical tone of

Optimism, *Certainty*, *Activity*, *Realism*, and *Commonality* used in social media by the largest revenue-grossing U.S. law firms. The dependent variables are defined in Appendix C.

Diction content analysis software was used because it is a methodical and objective method, according to Krippendorff (2013), and because it has been consistently used in prior OIM studies (Bravo et al., 2012; Craig & Brennan, 2012; Hall et al., 2012; Parhankangas & Ehrlich, 2012; Patelli & Pedrini, 2013; Tyler et al., 2012). Diction software was also used because dictionaries can control for issues such as inability to code similar terms, inter-rater reliability issues, and subjective coding. Diction has been used to analyze several types of organizational communications, and its dictionary is based on a collection of such narratives since the 1960s (Craig et al., 2013). Its robustness indicates empirical validity, and its automated analysis warrants measurement validity (Patelli & Pedrini, 2013).

Accordingly, Diction software was used to analyze law firm organizational Twitter postings for rhetorical tone. The population for this study was the 100 largest revenue-grossing law firms named in the *AmLaw 100* list (American Lawyer, 2013). A stratified, purposive sample of six law firms was chosen from the *AmLaw 100* list.

Criteria for inclusion in the study were firms based in the United States; actively using social media, such as Twitter; having specific litigation specialties for specialty type objectivity, and firms from each half of the upper and lower quartiles for financial objectivity.

Organizational postings on Twitter were downloaded, converted to .txt, processed through Diction software, exported to an Excel spreadsheet, and subsequently analyzed through SPSS to answer the research questions. Diction's output categorized the data and produced a numerical score of the five dependent variables. The researcher then exported the data to Excel and performed repeated measures ANOVA through SPSS. The results were presented in Chapter 4 and are further analyzed and interpreted in the current chapter. The outlier variables in Diction categories are addressed in comparison to Diction's Business Corporate Public Relations (BCPR) normative range. In addition, outlier variables are discussed in terms of their OIM implications and whether they are related to the OIM taxonomy. The remainder of Chapter 5 presents conclusions, implications, and recommendations for further study. The next section represents the findings from Diction's output and a subsequent analysis to answer the research questions.

Summary of Findings and Conclusion

The following section presents the results of this study grouped by research question, as in Chapter 4. The findings are based on Diction's output on the dependent variables, also known as Master Variables: *Certainty*, *Optimism*, *Activity*, *Realism*, and *Commonality*. The results and discussion of Diction's scores on the five Master Variables and outlier sub-variables are presented first, followed by interpretation of the statistical analysis based on Diction's numerical scores and in order of research question.

Alignment to OIM theory. Recent OIM studies that have used Diction for analysis of rhetorical tone, semantics, and other linguistic characteristics are summarized in Appendix D. Diction embodies rhetorical tone of messages that demonstrate OIM (Schniederjans et al., 2013). According to Goffman's (1959) theory, OIM involves controlling information in order to influence stakeholder's perceptions about an organization. Within the context of OIM theory and as measured by Diction, complexity, reading difficulty, and optimistic tone are examples of text manipulation that emphasize positive information and obfuscate negative information. While optimistic tone can be a form of sincerity, *Optimism* in OIM refers to emphasis on positive information while downplaying negative information (Patelli & Pedrini, 2013). Other researchers have used Diction to extract OIM themes as categorized in the OIM taxonomy (Mohamed et al., 1999). Still others have used Diction and discovered new OIM themes (Neuendorf, 2002; Parhankangas et al., 2012). In addition, Diction sub-variables of *Blame*, *Hardship*, *Deception*, *Aggression*, and *Embellishment* overlap with tactics in the OIM taxonomy. Thus, Diction has been successfully used to identify OIM strategies that may or may not be necessarily tied to the OIM taxonomy by Mohamed et al. (1999).

According to Krippendorff (2013), content analysis is a unique approach to data analysis. As a research technique, it is both replicable and valid through inferences from texts. In other words, research claims can be upheld through independently available evidence. Content analysis can be qualitative or quantitative in nature, but the main purpose is to explore textual content for manifest and latent meaning (Neuendorf, 2002). The requirements are that it be objective and systematic, which can be accomplished through use of unbiased, systematic content analysis software. This study used content analysis software that has been independently verified in previous OIM studies. Therefore, the study is replicable, and this type of content analysis has been validated in prior studies of this nature. The design for answering the research questions necessitated a quantitative study using a causal comparative research design, with historical content analysis (Krippendorff, 2013).

This study found slight differences among revenue categories, litigation specialty types, and yearly differences in rhetorical tone used in social media by law firms. The higher revenue firms exhibited higher levels of *Optimism* than firms in the lower quartile. The low revenue firms scored lower than Diction's normative range on average. This finding is consistent with Patelli and Pedrini (2013), who found a positive relationship between high *Optimism* and financial performance. Schniederjans et al. (2013) also found that revenue reflected high *Optimism*. The present study did not find that higher *Certainty* scores were representative of financial performance. However, Schniederjans et al. came to a different conclusion regarding *Certainty* and were able to correlate both *Optimism* and *Certainty* to financial performance.

Analysis of Diction scores. Diction's Master Variables served as the dependent variables in this study to measure rhetorical tone in law firm's Twitter posts over a 5-year period. The five Master Variables, consisting of *Activity, Optimism, Certainty, Realism,* and *Commonality,* have been interpreted as OIM behaviors in prior literature.

Prior studies have used Diction variables along with the Mohamed et al. (1999) OIM taxonomy to identify assertive and defensive themes (Avery & MacKay, 2006; Chilcutt, 2009; Nagy et al., 2012; O'Keefe & Conway, 2008; Parhankangas & Ehrlich, 2012; Pollach & Kerbler, 2011; Schniederjans et al., 2013; Tyler et al., 2012; Vielhaber & Waltman, 2008). Thus, researchers have related *Optimism* and *Certainty* in Diction software to assertive OIM behaviors (Patelli & Pedrini, 2013; Schniederjans et al., 2013).

The following analysis was conducted regarding rhetorical tone on organizational Twitter sites. The Master Variable *Activity* did not present many outlier scores in comparison to Diction's normative range. Product liability firms scored low in this variable in 2014, but this was not a significant difference. For *Optimism*, firm PL2 was the only firm scoring low, while the others were within the normative range. All firms consistently scored low on *Certainty* for each of the 5 years. As a group, all firms scored low in *Realism*, while firm PL2 scored within range for 4 of 5 years. Firm LL2 was the only firm that scored low on *Commonality* over each of the 5 years.

The use of *Optimism* in OIM theory refers to emphasis on positive information while downplaying negative information (Patelli & Pedrini, 2013). Optimistic tone is an example of text manipulation in order to emphasize the positive and can also be a form of sincerity. This study found that *Optimism* scores were higher for high revenue firms, confirming Patelli and Pedrini's (2013) findings. Patelli and Pedrini further surmised that positive tone, combined with good performance, was indicative of sincerity as well.

Praise, *Satisfaction*, and *Inspiration* are sub-variables that increase *Optimism*, Whereas *Blame*, *Hardship*, and *Denial* are sub-variables that decrease it (Hart, 2014).

The findings in this study concur with those of Tetlock et al. (2008), who studied news stories from the *S&P 500* and found that negativity often forecasted low firm earnings. In other words, stock market prices incorporate negative press information, and the stories predict both earnings and returns. The firms in the present study are representative of the largest revenue-grossing law firms in the United States that have appeared on a coveted industry list. The findings suggest that higher revenue-grossing firms have higher *Optimism* scores than firms in the lower quartile.

However, in contrast to Tetlock et al. (2008), Yuthas et al. (2002), and Patelli and Pedrini (2013), this study found that *Optimism* was within Diction's normative range for each firm over a 5-year period, with one exception. Firm PL2 showed lower *Optimism* levels than other firms and was lower than Diction's normative range for years 2010, 2011, 2013, and 2014. Thus, the *Optimism* scores, although higher for the higher revenues firms, fell within the normative range. This study did not find *Optimism* scores significantly different for the sample of high revenue firms on the *AmLaw 100* list. Nonetheless, higher scores on the upper quartile firms correspond to other findings that *Optimism* is connected to higher revenues. The interpretation, therefore, is that more optimistic messages, which include endorsements and highlighting of achievements, are equated with higher revenue firms in the upper quartile. The question remains whether higher revenue firms are more optimistic or, as findings in prior research studies suggested, optimistic messages are a way to attain higher revenues.

Certainty has been used in prior OIM research as a direct assertive variable. (Craig et al., 2013). Craig et al. (2013) used Diction Master Variable *Certainty* to measure deceptive content in corporate letters. They found that a high uncertainty score (i.e., low certainty) was associated with a high probability of deception. Diction calculates *Certainty* as [Tenacity + Leveling Terms + Collectives + Insistence] – [Numerical Terms + Ambivalence + Self Reference + Variety]. Accordingly, this study found that all six firms had low *Certainty* scores. While low scores may not indicate deception, they could indicate use of strategic OIM tactics to manipulate corporate image. It should also be noted that Craig et al. found lower use of *Self- reference* to be a high deception factor, although none of the firms scored outside of the normative range on that sub-variable in this study.

Moreover, Craig and Brennan (2012) measured reputation of firms on *Fortune* magazine's *America's Most Admired Companies* list using six Diction variables (Reputation = variety, inspiration, present concern, concreteness, complexity, realism [p.13]). A high score in *Realism* is indicative of verbiage concerning everyday matters that are immediate, familiar, and tangible to readers. Craig and Brennan tested "high reputation" firms to see if they had high scores in *Realism*, as was suggested in earlier research. Craig and Brennan found no association between *Realism* and corporate reputation, and this study also revealed that firms on the prestigious *AmLaw 100* list did not exhibit high *Realism*. In fact, 19 of 30 scores fell below the normative range in *Realism*, with only firm PL2 showing within-range normative scores for 4 out of 5 years.

The last Master Variable, *Commonality*, was not statistically significant among revenue for quartile or litigation specialty type. Of the 30 scores for the 5-year period, 12 were lower than Diction's normative range. Only firm LL2 consistently showed low *Commonality* scores over the 5-year period. Prior OIM research has indicated that high *Commonality* is positively associated with sincerity and financial performance (Patelli & Pedrini, 2013). Low scores among law firms could be a result of the nature of the industry. For example, *Commonality* indicates communication of agreed-upon group values and rejection of idiosyncratic models of engagement (Hart, 2014). The components of the variable are *Centrality*, *Cooperation*, and *Rapport* scores, minus *Diversity*, *Exclusion*, and *Liberation*. Upon examination of the sub-variables, the researcher found that 4 of the 6 firms scored low on *Rapport* and 2 scored extremely high on *Exclusion*. Perhaps due to the nature of the legal industry, law firms must use language that is unbiased, fact-based, and not indicative of any specific group values.

Aggregate results on sub-variables. Although not central to this study, Diction results for sub-variables are worth noting. All six firms scored extremely high on *Numerical Terms* and extremely low on *Familiarity*. All but firm PL2 scored extremely low on *Human Interest* and showed a different pattern than other firms. *Accomplishment, Ambivalence, Tenacity, Praise, Present Concern,* and *Leveling Terms* were other sub- variables that showed lower overall scores than the normative average collectively for all firms.

The high scores on *Numerical Terms* among all firms and for all years corresponds to the study by Craig et al. (2013), who found that reluctance to use numerical terms was consistent with deceptive conduct. The premise was that those using lower numerical terms do not want to arouse scrutiny of financial documents. Thus, excluding numerical terms is an OIM tactic of averting examination and managing external perceptions of stakeholders. In contrast, honesty is portrayed through specific, quantified claims. Craig et al. found a substantial difference between two companies that had high and low *Numerical Terms* scores. In fact, the CEO involved in a financial scam scored exceedingly low on Diction's *Numerical Terms* variable. The fact that firms in this study exhibited high *Numerical Terms* scores across social media may indicate sincerity and disclosure.

In the present study, the product liability firms scored low in *Centrality*. The interpretation is that firm's use of language indicated a tone of incongruence with standard values of society and atypical messages. According to Diction's definition, *Centrality* is a sign of systematic, ritualistic conformance to basic core values (see Appendix C). This finding is inconsistent with the expectation that law firms remain unbiased, systematic, and matter-of-fact. Perhaps law firms scored low on this variable in Twitter because they are confined to present communications succinctly.

The previous section presented the researcher's analysis of Diction scores in relation to other's findings. Interpretation of the aggregate scores in Diction provided a basis for answering the three research questions central to this study. The results and discussion are provided below and organized by research question.

Inferences from statistical analysis. Several inferences can be drawn based on the findings in this study. Research Question 1 asked, *Do differences exist in any of the five OIM strategy metrics based on revenue (bottom quartile versus top quartile)?* Although not statistically significant, *Certainty* scores for the upper quartile were $p = .06$, therefore statistically significant at a 90% confidence interval. The higher-revenue law firms tended to have higher levels of *Certainty*, which corresponds to prior research (Craig et al., 2013; Pollach & Kerbler, 2011). It seems fitting that firms at the top of the *AmLaw 100* list would exhibit higher levels of *Certainty*, indicating resoluteness, tenacity, self-reference, and embellishment. These factors have also been related to Direct Assertive behaviors on the OIM taxonomy (Pollach & Kerbler, 2011; Schniederjans et al., 2013). Based on this study, it can be concluded that higher-revenue law firms tend to portray language reflective of *Certainty* in their social media communications.

Other differences worth noting are that the upper quartile firms showed higher *Optimism* scores each year compared to the lower-revenue firms. Although the present study did not find a statistically significant difference, the Diction scores indicated that this study's findings agree with prior findings that higher *Optimism* equates to higher revenue (Patelli & Pedrini, 2013). In essence, higher *Optimism* is a component of Direct Assertive OIM behaviors in that an organization actively endorses its own causes, people, or events, and highlights its positive accomplishments. This behavior has been tied to the OIM act of embellishment, which is part of Direct Assertive behavior (Pollach & Kerbler, 2011; Schniederjans et al., 2013). The Diction scores for the sample in this study indicated that optimistic tone in social media communications was positively associated with higher revenues. Thus, it can be inferred that Direct Assertive behaviors, specifically *Optimism* and *Certainty*, are traits exhibited by higher revenue-producing law firms.

Embellishment is also a component of Diction's Master Variable *Activity*, as are *Accomplishment*, *Cognition*, and *Passivity*. While most firms scored low in Diction on these sub-variables, the overall scores on the Master Variable *Activity* were within Diction's normative range. *Embellishment* has been linked to the OIM defensive strategies of using prosocial claims. These claims are used by companies that need to maintain their reputational rankings. Some prosocial claims include (a) charity, (b) philanthropy, (c) disaster relief, (d) environmental protection, (e) promotion of education, (f) social justice, and (g) support of the arts. Organizations are apt to make prosocial claims to neutralize any negativity or reputational threats (McDonnell & King, 2013). The defense is unlike corporate social activity claims in the direct assertive OIM category.

Yet other researchers have stated that philanthropy and claims of social responsibility represent the OIM direct assertive category of exemplification (Pollach & Kerbler, 2011). Organizations flaunt corporate social activity, philanthropy, and associations with welfare organizations to gain prestige. This statement contradicts McDonnell and King (2013), who studied past behaviors used to buffer future reputational threats. Pollach and Kerbler (2011) studied CEO profiles as role models for organizational integrity. It is interesting to note that neither the upper- nor lower-revenue quartiles exhibited high *Activity* but, rather, fell within the normative range. Based on the findings of this study, high- and low-revenue firms displayed equal amounts of *Activity* in their social media communications.

While the variable *Activity* did not display any difference between firms, the upper quartile scored lower than the lower ranking firms on *Realism* and higher on *Commonality*. Patelli and Pedrini (2013) found that *Commonality* increases with the use of engaging language, which they tied to sincerity. Additionally, an increase in *Commonality* was found to be positively associated with financial performance (Patelli & Pedrini, 2013). The lower-revenue quartile firms in this study exhibited lower *Commonality* scores on average. The scores for the lower quartile were also lower than Diction's normative range. This finding agrees with that of Patelli and Pedrini, who found that organizations that use non-engaging language, indicative of low *Commonality* scores, are likely to have lower revenues than organizations with high *Commonality* scores. Based on the findings of this study, it is presumed that use of engaging language and group values, indicative of high *Commonality*, is an OIM strategy used by financially successful firms. Similarly, it can be deduced that successful firms avoid excessive use of ordinary, common, unremarkable language, representative of *Realism*, in their social media communications.

Although not central to this study, a discussion of Diction's sub-variables scores is in order. The firms in the upper quartile scored lower on *Ambivalence*, *Tenacity*, and *Blame* and higher on *Collectives*. According to OIM theory, the scores for these traits make sense, except for *Tenacity*, which includes definitive verb terms, confidence, and totality. However, the results of this study indicate that higher revenue firms are more concrete in their communications, hence appearing less ambivalent and not shifting blame to others. The results of the sub-variables are in line with Direct Assertive behavior in OIM theory. Thus, the findings of this study agree with prior research linking Direct Assertive strategies to higher revenue (Patelli & Pedrini, 2013, Pollach & Kerbler, 2011; Schniederjans et al., 2013).

Hence, this study established the existence of differences in law firm's social media OIM strategies based on revenue. Likewise, the researcher attempted to explore whether rhetorical tone differences existed based on litigation specialty. Research Question 2 stated, *Do differences exist in any of the five OIM strategy metrics based on specialty (labor law versus intellectual property versus product liability)?*

The findings of this study showed no significant differences on the five OIM metrics among the three litigation specialties. However, the PL firm's Diction scores varied from the other two specialty categories. All firms scored lower than the normative average on *Certainty*, but the PL firms scored lowest. They also scored lower than Diction's normative range and lower than the other specialties on *Optimism*. Along with the other categories, they scored low on *Realism*.

As the researcher analyzed the sub-variables to compare other differences, it became clear that the Diction scores for the PL firms were inconsistent across several variables. Firm PL2 showed patterns that were out of range from both its specialty type and other firms, with outliers in several key areas. A statistically significant difference, according to Yuthas et al. (2002), includes scores that vary more than 2% on Master Variables and more than 20% on sub-variables. Firm PL2 scored extremely high in *Blame* (333%) and *Hardship* (109%) in Twitter. Although within range, it was the highest scoring firm on *Aggression*.

Moreover, firm PL2 was unusual in many respects and the only firm to score extremely high on two defensive variables. Negative tone and use of personal pronouns have been tied to OIM defensive behaviors (Craig et al., 2013; Vielhaber & Waltman, 2008). According to Vielhaber and Waltman (2008), defensive strategies included (a) attacks on the accuser, (b) denial, (c) excuses, and (d) justification, which includes *Blame* and *Hardship*. Apology and justifications are considered defensive and proactive strategies to defend image (Schniederjans et al., 2013). Firm PL2 also scored high on *Variety*, which represents an avoidance of overstatement and use of more complex phrases. According to Craig and Brennan (2012), low *Variety* indicates a more relaxed writing style and perhaps higher credibility. The extreme scores on *Blame*, *Hardship*, and *Variety* variables can perhaps be attributed to litigation type, since firm PL2 was the only PL firm in the *AmLaw 100* list that specifically litigated in medical malpractice.

The IP firms scored within Diction's normative range but higher on *Optimism* and *Commonality* than the other two specialties. This result implies that, in line with prior OIM research, these firms express optimistic, conversant language that exemplifies group values. As with other firms in this study, the IP forms scored lower in *Certainty* and *Realism*, which have been linked to illusory behaviors but more than likely are a reflection of flexibility. Intellectual property firms in general must strive to uphold agreed-upon values, hence high scores on *Commonality*, and perhaps must use more complicated dialogue due to the nature of their work.

Two sub-variables that stood out were *Concreteness* and *Present Concern*, both scoring much higher than normal in Diction. Again, this result most likely reflects the nature of the work involved with intellectual property law. Use of definitive terms, present tense verbs, and materiality are all sub-components of the Master Variable *Realism*. However, the extremely high scores on these sub-variables were not enough to raise the *Realism* score in general.

Interestingly, firm IP1 was extremely high in *Concreteness* (102%) and *Past Concern* (203%) in Twitter, using Yuthas et al.'s (2002) method of statistical significance on variation from Diction normative scores. The *Concreteness* variable is representative of tangibility and materiality (Hart, 2014). It possesses no utility other than representing language of nouns, units, or people in a straightforward manner. Per Craig and Brennan (2012), textual content of high reputation firms demonstrates straightforwardness and a matter-of-fact style. Firm IP1 scored extremely out-of-range (102%) on this particular sub-variable; perhaps this is one reason it is in the upper quartile, versus firm IP2 in the bottom quartile.

The last category, LL firms, scored low on *Certainty*, *Realism*, and *Commonality* in general. In *Commonality*, they scored lower than the others and lower than Diction's normative range. In the sub-variables, the LL firms scored low on *Praise*, a major component in Diction's Master Variable *Optimism*. LL firms were low in *Rapport* and *Present Concern* as well. According to prior OIM research, high reputation firms use present tense to exemplify what they are doing, in contrast to low reputation firms that imply what they attempt to do (Craig & Brennan, 2012). Craig and Brennan (2012) did not find this to be true, and neither did the present study. The LL firms that scored low on *Present Concern* are implicitly high reputation firms due to their names being on a coveted industry list. In particular, firm LL2 was extremely high in *Insistence* (342%), a statistically significant variation according to Yuthas et al. (2002).

Concluding this section is a discussion of results from the last research question, *Do differences exist in any of the five OIM strategy metrics based on year (2010 through 2014)?* The researcher took the average scores each year for each firm and compared 5- year differences among the five OIM metrics. This study found a statistically significant difference in *Activity* between years 2011 and 2014. The difference between years 2010 and 2014 was not statistically significant at $p = .058$. *Activity* scores were higher in 2011, perhaps due to the economic downturn in the mortgage and housing industries. In particular, the PL firms scored lowest in *Activity* in 2014. *Activity* reflects accomplishment, motion, communication, and aggressive behavior. Words tend to express task completion through a variety of social purposes (Hart, 2014). Given the state of the economy in 2011 compared to 2014, law firms were prepared to use action words to stimulate consumer engagement in tougher economic times.

In all 5 years, each firm scored low on *Certainty* and *Realism*, with no statistically significant difference among years 2010-2014. The implication of low scores on these metrics was discussed earlier. Additionally, firm PL2 was lowest on *Optimism* for 4 out of 5 years. The score was within Diction's normative range but lower than the other firms and second lowest in 2010. This result could reflect the nature of the product liability interests of firm PL2, which are based solely in medical malpractice. The results of sub-variables for firm PL2 showed higher *Aggression*, *Blame*, and *Hardship*; therefore, it would stand to reason that this firm would have less optimistic organizational communications.

Lastly, the *Commonality* scores for all firms were low in 2010 and 2012. Although the scores were lower than Diction's normative range, this study did not find a statistically significant difference in *Commonality* scores over a 5-year period. Basically, firms did not feel the need to adjust their messages based on use of language that reflects agreed-upon group values. Thus, the only finding was that *Activity* differed in Twitter messages more than the other four OIM metrics used in this study. It can be concluded, therefore, that in volatile economic times, successful firms tend to exhibit higher *Activity* in their social media communications, represented by aggressive language featuring change, accomplishment, motion, and avoidance of inertia.

Implications

As a result of this research, practitioners and researchers should examine the effectiveness of OIM strategies used in social media by successful law firms. The purpose of this quantitative, causal comparative study was to establish if there are differences in social media OIM strategies based on financial performance and litigation specialty by the largest revenue-grossing U.S. law firms. The OIM strategies used in social media by successful firms can offer guidance to others when formulating their strategies. Prior research has relied on identification of successful firms through their appearance on desirable industry lists, such as the *AmLaw 100* (McDonnell & King,2013). According to Goffman's (1959) dramaturgical self-presentation theory, organizations try to attain approval, status, and prestige from various stakeholders through use of OIM strategies (Highhouse et al., 2009). This goal is often achieved via corporate communications strategically managed to control information for the purpose of influencing stakeholder's perceptions.

While this study added to the body of knowledge on OIM, several limitations must addressed. The study confirmed the findings of prior research that higher revenue- grossing firms scored higher on *Optimism* but found no difference in OIM metrics among law firm specialty types. There was one significant difference on the variable *Activity* between years 2011 and 2014 among all law firms collectively.

The main weakness of this study was the sample selection. The findings could be skewed due to the population choice, since all firms appeared on the prestigious *AmLaw 100* list. In addition, the firms used in the study were from the 2013 list, and in a volatile economy, rankings can rapidly change. The sample chosen was limited to U.S. law firms, without consideration of global law firms on the *AmLaw 100* list. The use of quartiles could have presented a problem with adequately calculating differences from top and bottom revenue firms, since there was such a vast difference in revenues (McDonnell & King, 2013).

In the interest of time constraints, this study explored Twitter accounts of a stratified purposive sample of the largest revenue-grossing U.S. law firms. Content analysis on the social media sites of all 100 law firms would have taken a considerably longer amount of time. In addition, research was limited to one social media site in particular. Different social media may have varied in tone, depending on the site. This study was done on *tweets*, which are limited to 140 characters that originated from law firms. Therefore, the messages had to be brief, concise, and direct. This fact could have had an impact on the findings of this study. Future studies should consider other social media sites used by law firms.

In addition to brevity of Twitter messages, a weakness in this study is that it relied on quantitative analysis. A main assumption in this study was that quantitative content analysis adequately identified OIM strategies. Although use of software can be more subjective than hand coding (Krippendorff, 2013), qualitative studies often provide richer context and detect subtle nuances that computer software cannot (Brennan et al., 2008). This study was limited to the variables defined by the software. In some cases, content analysis software may not reflect the OIM categories in the taxonomy by Mohamed et al. (1999). Lastly, the researcher relied on Direct Assertive and Direct Defensive tactics as outlined in the Mohamed et al. taxonomy without regard for other OIM taxonomies that may exist.

On the other hand, the relevance and timeliness of exploring OIM strategies within social media was a key strength of this study. Organizations are increasingly using social media as a primary communication tool. The body of literature supports that social media research is limited, especially on rhetorical tone of messages as they relate to OIM strategies. Specifically, this study introduced the importance of maintaining organizational image via one of the most popular social media sites.

Although qualitative analysis may have delivered richer data and found textual subtleties, some doubt could remain about the study's objectivity. In other words, the use of an objective tool to quantify variables for further analysis can be considered a chief strength of this study. Prior studies have proven Diction software a valid and reliable tool for rhetorical tone analysis (Patelli & Pedrini, 2013). The researcher relied on rhetorical tone categories that have been used in other studies without fear of subjectivity or researcher bias.

A major constraint for most studies is that research is limited to an industry or top company lists. While this study was confined to the legal industry, it not only added to the body of OIM research across industries, but it also was the first study on social media OIM strategies of successful law firms. Industry choice can be considered both a strength and weakness when trying to equate findings from prior research studies. Therefore, another explanation for differences from prior research could revolve around industry choice. For example, Schniederjans et al. (2013) studied the OIM strategies of pharmaceutical firms and found Direct Assertive strategies to build image were used across social media in blogs, forums, and organizational web sites. The findings in the present study may be different because law firms behave differently than pharmaceutical firms, and Twitter messages differ from other types of social media. In contrast, Patelli and Pedrini (2013) studied the OIM strategies of *Fortune 500* firms from 15 industries and found through ANOVA that the OIM variables had statistically significant differences across industries.

Legally regulated content, such as legal communications or those that can be construed as legal communications, reflect the constraints of the particular group, which may present a problem in extracting OIM themes from law firm's social media sites. The OIM themes may be hidden or latent in comparison to more obvious and manifest content from other types of organizations. Therefore, the present study should be replicated using organizations from different industries.

Theoretical implications. The interpretation of the present findings is in line with Goffman's (1959) dramaturgical self-presentation theory. Like most organizations, law firms try to control, maintain, and manipulate their image to their publics. On social media sites, such as Twitter, the task proves more difficult because of the verbiage constraints and legal implications of posting what could be construed as legal advice.

This research focused solely on one-way organizational communications without regard for impression management perceptions from clients or other stakeholders.

As with Brennan et al. (2008), the user's perspective was not considered; therefore, the question of whether impression management techniques were successful was not measured. This study did not address whether stakeholders were influenced by OIM strategies, if their perceptions changed because of them, or if they discount OIM in social media in general.

However, this study did agree with prior researchers that higher optimism conveyance was positively related to higher revenues (Patelli & Pedrini, 2013). The implication for social media managers, and law firms particularly, is that creation of optimistic messages on social media could equate to higher revenue generation. Although all firms scored low on *Realism*, the higher revenue firms posted more messages indicative of immediate, everyday matters. Perhaps language indicating familiarity resonates with consumers looking to purchase legal services. Similarly, although *Commonality* scores were low among all firms, they were lower among the lower quartile over 5 years, implying that messages featuring core group values enhance the revenue- generating potential of social media messages.

Practical implications. The study of OIM has important implications since gaining the support of stakeholders is critical for most organizations (Tyler et al., 2012). Company images are often conveyed via public communications, such as social media, press releases, and annual reports. Therefore, it is important to understand which OIM tactics will help improve company image. It is important for organizations to realize the impressions they develop with either presence or absence of particular content in their social media (Pollach & Kerbler, 2011). As in this study, other studies have noted that the social significance attached to social media communications could be different in other industries.

Scholars of OIM need to explore the role of specific professional actors in shaping institutional standards and the ways they carry out projects in a group context (Lamertz & Martens, 2011). Lamertz and Martens (2011) found that images for organizations experiencing IPOs are significantly shaped by law firms that assert Direct Assertive dominance on the IPO prospectus. Given that law firms help shape images of other firms, it is only fitting that the study of law firm's OIM behaviors will lend insight to other practitioners on successful strategies. This study found that *Optimism* and *Commonality* were factors of higher-revenue law firms. This practical implication should be applied to law firms and could be used in other industries as well.

Future implications. A limitation of this study was that it was focused on one industry. Just as Avery and MacKay (2006) stated that it might be helpful to look at OIM tactics in areas other than recruitment, this research could be extended beyond the *AmLaw 100* list to include other law firms. Future studies may also look beyond OIM strategies used in social media and relate them to firm performance, as did Schniederjans et al. (2013) and Patelli and Pedrini (2013). Further, this study could follow Chilcutt (2009) to test the use of Assertive and Defensive strategies according to their relationship to customer satisfaction.

The present study did not find any statistically significant differences among law firms of different litigation specialties, and future studies could choose other litigation categories not considered in the present study. It could be that the legal industry in general has a proclivity to convey images in a certain way, perhaps due to ethical compliance. Similarly, a cross section of social media could be examined for variations in OIM usage over a lengthier period than 5 years. Overall, the findings in this study confirmed that firms projecting *Optimism* were more likely to produce higher revenues than firms not projecting *Optimism*. Those in the legal industry may find it helpful to maintain an optimistic tone in social media messages, convey core societal values in the essence of commonality, and maintain a realistic tone to enhance overall image among stakeholders.

Recommendations

Based on the study findings, it is recommended that practitioners and researchers explore other industries and types of social media. Although the study confirmed the findings of prior research, mainly that *Optimism* is associated with higher earnings, the study should be replicated with a larger sample and across different types of organizations. In addition, other OIM models and types of linguistic analysis software should be considered.

Recommendations for future research. Despite the findings of past literature and the present study, some questions remain unanswered. Therefore, future research should address questions such as the following: Will the study differ across industries and across varied social media? Will these findings persist in spite of different expectations by clients, assuming clients are sensitive to OIM strategies in law firm's social media? Would other software programs for language analysis provide better OIM analysis? Lastly, can the study be replicated using a different design approach?

The purpose of this study was to examine the social media OIM strategies of successful law firms to see identify any differences based on revenue and litigation type. A primary goal was to assist firms in effectively managing their organizational impressions to stakeholders. Future research can expand upon the present study through replication, using successful firms in other industries in order to compare their OIM strategies via Twitter. Additionally, this study could be expanded across different types of social media, such as law firm blogs.

Furthermore, given the reciprocal nature of social media, it would be prudent to conduct future research on consumer's perspectives of organizational postings on social media sites. Such a study may address whether clients are sensitive to law firm's social media OIM strategies. The power of consumers and other stakeholders, combined with the power of social media, has made it that much more important for organizations to carefully craft their public image (Brennan et al., 2013). Therefore, future researchers can conduct similar studies using the consumer perspective as a gauge for OIM effectiveness.

Another area for future research would be the use of other linguistic analysis programs. This study was limited to analysis of rhetorical tone categories found in Diction software. Future researchers should consider conducting a similar study using other programs or qualitative analysis for a richer exploration of textual content.

It is assumed that a larger sample size would have improved the present study; however, due to time constraints, the focus was on units of Twitter messages instead of number of firms. Indeed, the use of focus groups to include the client viewpoint could have provided a truer picture of whether OIM strategies achieved their intended purpose. Just as Tyler et al. (2012) suggested that the OIM model be tested in other industries and different types of organizations, the present study should be extended to include image projection on stakeholders. By expanding OIM studies in social media, researchers can find consistent themes in messages and the right technological options for communications (Vielhaber & Waltman, 2008).

Recommendations for practice. In general, researchers and practitioners can use the results of this study to rethink their OIM strategies in social media communications. The study results have tied OIM strategies used by law firms to the OIM taxonomy used by other researchers (Chilcutt, 2009). The study of OIM strategies provides organizations with ways to control public impressions and maintain organizational self-presentation.

This research suggests that OIM is pervasive in organizational communications via social media, and successful organizations display more optimistic messages (*Optimism*) focused on group values (*Commonality*). This study also found that organizations use multiple OIM strategies to exaggerate positive qualities about themselves and downplay negative information.

Specifically, this study's findings are significant for law firms. According to *The American Lawyer* magazine, law firms in the top 100 ranking billed more hours and pulled in higher fees, even as the economy slowed the overall demand for legal services in the second quarter of 2013 (*American Lawyer*, 2013). Accordingly, law firms in the second 100 ranking (*AmLaw 200*) did better overall than other U.S. law firms in terms of demand for and payment of legal services. Therefore, the study of the top revenue- grossing law firms and their OIM strategies via social media can provide a benchmark for those seeking to increase their financial standing.

In summary, Chapter 1 introduced the problem statement central to this study: It is not known if there are differences in social media OIM strategies based on financial performance and litigation specialty by the largest revenue-grossing U.S. law firms. Although law firms may be hesitant to use social media due to legal and ethical constraints, studies have shown increased use of social media among them (Vinson,2010). The purpose of this causal comparative quantitative study was to determine if differences existed in social media OIM strategies based on financial performance and litigation specialty among the largest revenue-grossing U.S. law firms. The present study addressed deficiencies in OIM research in social media and across industries and contributed to the literature through the study of OIM strategies used by successful law firms on social media site Twitter, which was chosen because of its popularity among law firms and the abundance of posts.

Moreover, the literature review in Chapter 2 covered Goffman's (1959) dramaturgical self-presentation theory to explain the motivations behind human social behavior. *Impression management* is defined as the process by which an individual "actor" attempts to manipulate, influence, or maintain his or her image to others (Chilcutt, 2009). Goffman surmised that organizations, like individuals, are concerned with self-presentation. Organizational motives for OIM are to enhance company image and brand, maintain reputation, and manage stakeholder's perceptions, while combatting negative image (Chilcutt, 2009; Highhouse et al., 2009; Tyler et al., 2012). While prior researchers have studied OIM through traditional media, the present study contributed to OIM theory by exploring the strategies used by successful firms via social media.

Moreover, the quantitative methodology described in Chapter 3 was necessary to answer the research questions. The three research questions and associated hypotheses addressed the differences in OIM strategies based on revenues, litigation specialty, and year. Following prior OIM studies, this study used Diction software to measure rhetorical tone of five variables. This causal comparative, quantitative study utilized an historical content analysis of law firm's Twitter sites. The researcher analyzed nearly 10,000 tweets posted by six purposefully selected law firms over a 5-year period. The researcher used repeated measures ANOVA for statistical analysis of OIM strategies as measured by rhetorical tone.

The results presented in Chapter 4 showed there were some differences in OIM strategies based on revenue. Although no statistically significant differences were found among the five dependent variables, *Certainty* scores for the upper revenue quartile were higher and nearly significant at $p = .06$. This finding is in agreement with prior researchers who concluded that high *Certainty* scores are related to higher financial performance (Craig et al., 2013; Pollach & Kerbler, 2011). Similarly, the upper quartile firms showed higher *Optimism* scores each year compared to the lower-revenue firms, although the scores were not statistically significant. The findings agree with prior research linking high *Optimism* scores to higher revenue (Patelli & Pedrini, 2013).

Conversely, this study found no statistically significant differences on the five OIM metrics among the three litigation specialties. However, this study found that the PL firm's rhetorical tone scores varied considerably from the other two specialty categories. Product Liability firms scored lowest on *Certainty, Optimism,* and *Realism.* The speculation is that PL firms in general are more aggressive in nature, depending on specialization type. In this case, one of the firms was a top medical malpractice litigator. The average scores across the OIM variables were affected by the extreme scores exhibited by this one firm.

Lastly, this study found a statistically significant difference in *Activity* between years 2011 and 2014 ($p = .040$) and a substantial difference between years 2010 and 2014 ($p = .058$). *Activity* scores were higher in 2011, perhaps due to the economic downturn in the mortgage and housing industries. All firms over 5 years scored low in *Certainty* and *Realism,* with no statistically significant difference among years 2010-2014. However, an interesting finding was that PL firms scored lowest in *Activity* in 2014, and one PL firm scored lowest on *Optimism* 4 out of 5 years. This result could reflect the medical malpractice specialization of firm PL2. This firm in particular showed outlier scores in several sub-variables, such as *Aggression, Blame,* and *Hardship.* Although this study did not find differences based on litigation specialty, this finding warrants more research on differences in OIM strategies based on specialty type. Researchers can examine if PL firms do indeed have less optimistic organizational communications or if this result was a by-product of social media as the vehicle.

References

Alvarez, G., Dalton, B., Lamport, J., & Tsamis, K. (2014). *The social law firm: An assessment of the use of social technologies at America's leading law firms.* Retrieved from http://good2bsocial.com/2014/01/22/social-media-rankings-top- law-firms/American Lawyer. (2013, May 10). The AmLaw 100. *The American Lawyer.*

Avery, D. R., & McKay, P. F. (2006). Target practice: An organizational impression management approach to attracting minority and female job applicants. *Personnel Psychology, 59*(1), 157–187. doi:10.1111/j.1744-6570.2006.00807.x

Barnes, N., Lescault, A., & Wright, S. (2013). 2013 Fortune 500 are bullish on social media: Big companies get excited about Google+, Instagram, Foursquare and Pinterest. *University of Massachusetts Dartmouth Center for Marketing Research.* Retrieved from http://www.umassd.edu/cmr/socialmediaresearch/2013fortune500/Baskervil le Watkins, M., Smith, A., & Aquino, K. (2013). The use and consequences of strategic sexual performances. *Academy of Management Perspectives, 27*(3), 173–186. doi:10.5465/amp.2010.0109

Becker, T. E., & Martin, S. L. (1995). Trying to look bad at work: Methods and motives for managing poor impressions in organizations. *Academy of Management Journal, 38*(1), 174–199. doi:10.2307/256732

Bobowski, K. (2014, April 18). Are your social problems legally compliant? [Web log post]. Retrieved from https://smartblogs.com/social-media/2014/04/18/are-your- social-promotions-legally-compliant/

Bolino, M. C. (1999). Citizenship and impression management: Good soldiers or good actors? *Academy of Management Review, 24*(1), 82–98. doi:10.5465/ AMR.1999.1580442

Bolino, M. C., Kacmar, K. M., Turnley, W. H., & Gilstrap, J. B. (2008). A multi-level review of impression management motives and behaviors. *Journal of Management, 34*(6), 1080–109. doi:10.1177/0149206308324325

Bolino, M. C., & Turnley, W. H. (1999). Impression management in organizations: A scale development based on the Pittman taxonomy. *Organizational Research Methods, 2*(2), 187–206.

Boyd, D., & Ellison, N. (2007). Social network sites: Definition, history, and scholarship.

Journal of Computer-Mediated Communication, 13(1), 210–230. doi:10.1111/j.1083-6101.2007.00393.x

Bravo, R., Matute, J., & Pina, J. M. (2012). Corporate social responsibility as a vehicle to reveal the corporate identity: A study focused on the websites of Spanish financial entities. *Journal of Business Ethics, 107*(2),129–146. doi:10.1007/s10551-011-1027-2

Brennan, N. M., Guillamón-Saorín, E., & Pierce, A. (2008). Impression management: Developing and illustrating a scheme of analysis for narrative disclosures—A methodological note. *Accounting, Auditing, & Accountability Journal.*

Retrieved from ttp://papers.ssrn.com/sol3/papers.cfm?abstract_id=1284904

Brennan, N. M., Merkl-Davies, D. M., & Beelitz, A. (2013). Dialogism in corporate social responsibility communications: Conceptualising verbal interaction between organisations and their audiences. *Journal of Business Ethics, 115*(4), 665–679. doi:10.1007/s10551-013-1825-9

Carlson, J., Carlson, D., & Ferguson, M. (2010). Deceptive impression management: Does deception pay in established workplace relationships? *Journal of Business Ethics, 100*(3), 497–514. doi:10.1007/s10551-010-0693-9

Chang, C. (2008). To donate or not to donate? Product characteristics and framing effects of cause-related marketing on consumer purchase behavior. *Psychology & Marketing, 25*(12), 1089–110. doi:10.1002/mar.20255

Chilcutt, A. S. (2009). The "reality" of Southwest: A content analysis of managing organizational impression tactics during a season of "Airline." *Public Relations Journal, 3*(3).

Craig, R., & Brennan, N. M. (2012). An exploration of the relationship between language choice in CEO letters to shareholders and corporate reputation. *Accounting Forum, 36*(3), 166–177. doi:10.1016/j.accfor.2012.02.004

Craig, R., Mortensen, T., & Iyer, S. (2013). Exploring top management language for signals of possible deception: The words of Satyam's Chair Ramalinga Raju.

Journal of Business Ethics, 113(2), 333–347. doi:10.1007/s10551-012-1307-5

Dayton, A. (2013, Sept. 16). You read it here: Blogs never sleep. *National Law Journal.* Retrieved from http://www.nationallawjournal.com/id=1202619190022/You-Read-It-Here%3A-Blogs-Never-Sleep#ixzz2v14mJdOM

Demay, J. E. (2011). The implications of the social media revolution on discovery in U.S. litigation. *The Brief, 40*(4), 55–64. Retrieved from http://search.proquest.com/ docview/878528988?accountid=7374

Devlin, A. S. (2006). *Research methods: Planning, conducting and presenting research.*

Belmont, CA: Thomson/Wadsworth.

Doohwang, L., Hyuk Soo, K., & Jung Kyu, K. (2011). The impact of online brand community type on consumer's community engagement behaviors: Consumer- created vs. marketer-created online brand community in online social-networking web sites. *Cyberpsychology, Behavior & Social Networking, 14*(1/2), 59–63. doi:10.1089/cyber.2009.0397

Du, S., Bhattacharya, C. B., & Sen, S. (2010). Maximizing business returns to corporate social responsibility (CSR): The role of CSR in communication. *International Journal of Management Reviews, 12*(1), 8–19. doi:10.1111/j.1468-2370.2009.00276.x

Ellison, N., Steinfield, C., & Lampe, C. (2007). The benefits of Facebook "friends": Social capital and college student's use of online social network sites. *Journal of Computer-Mediated Communication, 12*(4), 1143–168. doi:10.1111/j.1083-6101.2007.00367.x

Fairley, S. (2013, Aug. 29). ABA survey says lawyers getting clients via social media.

National Law Review. Retrieved from http://www.natlawreview.com/article/ aba-survey-says-lawyers-getting-clients-social-media

Ferraro, R., Kirmani, A., & Matherly, T. (2013). Look at me! Look at me! Conspicuous brand usage, self-brand connection, and dilution. *Journal of Marketing Research, 50*(4), 477–488. doi:10.1509/jmr.11.0342

Goffman, E. (1959). *The presentation of self in everyday life.* Garden City, NY: Doubleday.

Gravetter, F. J., & Wallnau, L. B. (2013). *Statistics for the behavioral sciences* (9th ed.).

Belmont, CA: Wadsworth.

Gurevitch, Z. D. (1985). The receiver's dilemma: Impressions formed in response to impression management. *Basic & Applied Social Psychology, 6*(2), 145–157. doi:10.1207/s15324834basp0602_4

Hale, D. (2010). Social networking: The new marketing channel. *Journal of Business Management and Entrepreneurship, 1*(9). Retrieved from http://www.theelearninginstitute.org/journal_pdf/JOBME%20-%20Social%20Networking%20-20The%20New%20Marketing%20Channel.pdf

Halim, H., & Jaafar, H. (2012). Intangibles disclosure and capital-raising in Australia: An analysis of information intensity. *Asian Academy of Management Journal of Accounting & Finance, 8*(2), 69–91.

Hall, J. A., Pennington, N., & Lueders, A. (2013). Impression management and formation on Facebook: A lens model approach. *New Media & Society, 15*(6), 1–25. doi:10.1177/1461444813495166

Hambrick, M. E., Simmons, J. M., Greenhalgh, G. P., & Greenwell, T. C. (2010). Understanding professional athlete's use of Twitter: A content analysis of athlete tweets. *International Journal of Sport Communication, 3*(4), 454–471.

Harris, K. J., Gallagher, V. C., & Rossi, A. (2013). Impression management (IM)behaviors, IM culture, and job outcomes. *Journal of Managerial Issues, 25*(2),154–171.

Hart, R. (2014). Diction (Version 7.0): The text analysis program [Computer software].Retrieved from http://www.dictionsoftware.com/

Highhouse, S., Brooks, M. E., & Gregarus, G. (2009). An organizational impression management perspective on the formation of corporate reputations. *Journal of Management, 35*(6), 1481–493. doi:10.1177/0149206309348788

Huang, S. Y., Huang, S. M., Wu, T. H., & Hsieh, T. Y. (2011). The data quality evaluation of graph information. *Journal of Computer Information Systems, 51*(4), 81–91.

Hyun Ju, J., & Mira, L. (2013). The effect of online media platforms on joining causes: The impression management perspective. *Journal of Broadcasting & Electronic Media, 57*(4), 439–455. doi:10.1080/08838151.2013.845824

Jin, S., & Lee, K. (2010). The influence of regulatory fit and interactivity on brand satisfaction and trust in e-health marketing inside 3D virtual worlds (second life). *Cyberpsychology, Behavior & Social Networking, 13*(6), 673–680. doi:10.1089/ cyber.2009.0292

Jones, E., & Pittman, T. (1982). Toward a general theory of strategic self-presentation. In J. Suls (Ed.), *Psychological perspectives on the self* (pp. 231–261). Hillsdale, NJ: Erlbaum.

Kacmar, K., Harris, K., & Nagy, B. (2007). Further validation of the Bolino and Turnley impression management scale. *Journal of Behavioral & Applied Management, 9*(1), 16–32.

Karl, K. A., McIntyre Hall, L., & Peluchette, J. V. (2013). City employee perceptions of the impact of dress and appearance: You are what you wear. *Public Personnel Management, 42*(3), 452–470. doi:10.1177/0091026013495772

Klaman, B., & Oreskovic, A. (2012, May 15). GM to drop Facebook ads due to low consumer impact. *Reuters*. Retrieved from http://www.reuters.com/article/2012/05/15/net-us-gm-facebook-idUSBRE84E1D420120515

Krippendorff, K. (2013). *Content analysis: An introduction* (3rd ed.). Los Angeles, CA.Sage.

Kucuk, S. (2010). Negative double jeopardy revisited: A longitudinal analysis. *Journal of Brand Management, 18*(2), 150–158. doi:10.1057/bm.2010.27

Kwok, L. (2012). Exploratory-triangulation design in mixed methods studies: A case of examining graduating seniors who meet hospitality recruiter's selection criteria. *Tourism and Hospitality Research, 12*(3), 125–138.

Kwok, L., & Yu, B. (2013). Spreading social media messages on Facebook: An analysis of restaurant business-to-consumer communications. *Cornell Hospitality Quarterly, 54*(1), 84–94. doi:10.1177/1938965512458360

Lai, C., Chiu, C., Yang, C., & Pai, D. (2010). The effects of corporate social responsibility on brand performance: The mediating effect of industrial brand equity and corporate reputation. *Journal of Business Ethics, 95*(3), 457–469. doi:10.1007/s10551-010-0433-1

Lamertz, K., & Martens, M. L. (2011). How do we make you look good? A social network study of upstream organizational impression management and the rhetorical construction of IPO firm images. *Canadian Journal of Administrative Sciences, 28*(4), 373. doi:10.1002/cjas.193

Leary, M., & Kowalski, R. (1990). Impression management: A literature review and two- component model. *Psychological Bulletin, 107*(1), 34–47. doi:10.1037/0033- 2909.107.1.34

LexisNexis. (2014a). *Examining the future for law firms and social media.* Retrieved from http:/ www.martindale-hubbell.co.uk/socialmedia

LexisNexis. (2014b). *Global social media check up: A global audit of law firm engagement in social media methods.* Retrieved from http://www.martindale- hubbell.co.uk/socialmedia

Lovejoy, K., Waters, R. D., & Saxton, G. D. (2012). Engaging stakeholders through Twitter: How nonprofit organizations are getting more out of 140 characters or less. *Public Relations Review, 38*(2), 313–318. doi:10.1016/j.pubrev.2012.01.005

Matejek, S., & Gössling, T. (2014). Beyond legitimacy: A case study in BP's "green lashing." *Journal of Business Ethics, 120*(4), 571–584. doi:10.1007/s10551-013- 2006-6

Mathioudakis, M., & Koudas, N. (2010, June). Twittermonitor: Trend detection over the twitter stream. In *Proceedings of the 2010 ACM SIGMOD International Conference on Management of Data* (pp. 1155–158). West Lafayette, IN: ACM.

McDonnell, M., & King, B. (2013). Keeping up appearances: Reputational threat and impression management after social movement boycotts. *Administrative Science Quarterly, 58*(3), 387–419. doi:10.1177/0001839213500032

Merkl-Davies, D.M., & Brennan, N. (2007). Discretionary disclosure strategies in corporate narratives: Incremental information or impression management? *Journal of Accounting Literature, 26*, 116–196.

Michelon, G. G. (2011). Sustainability disclosure and reputation: A comparative study. *Corporate Reputation Review, 14*(2), 79–96. doi:10.1057/crr.2011.10

Miller, C. C. (2009, August 25). Who's driving Twitter's popularity? Not teens. *The New York Times.* Retrieved from http://www.nytimes.com/2009/08/26/technology/nternet/26twitter.html?em

Miller, M., Wood, S., Sicafuse, L., & Chomos, J. (2010, June 1). The impact of juror's perceptions of attorneys and their performance on verdict. *Social Science Research Network.* doi:10.2139/ssrn.1633237

Mohamed, A., Gardner, W., & Paolillo, J. (1999). A taxonomy of organizational impression management tactics. *Advances in Competitiveness Research, 7*(1), 108–130.

Muthukrishnan, A., & Chattopadhyay, A. (2007). Just give me another chance: The strategies for brand recovery from a bad first impression. *Journal of Marketing Research, 44*(2), 334–345. doi:10.1509/jmkr.44.2.334

Nagy, B., Kacmar, M., & Harris, K. (2011). Dispositional and situational factors as predictors of impression management behaviors. *Journal of Behavioral and Applied Management, 12*(3), 229–245. doi:2373068381

Nagy, B. G., Pollack, J. M., Rutherford, M. W., & Lohrke, F. T. (2012). The influence of entrepreneur's credentials and impression management behaviors on perceptions of new venture legitimacy. *Entrepreneurship: Theory & Practice, 36*(5), 941– 965. doi:10.1111/j.1540-6520.2012.00539.x

Neuendorf, K. A. (2002). *The content analysis guidebook.* Thousand Oaks, CA: Sage.

O'Keefe, P., & Conway, S. (2008). *Impression management and legitimacy in an NGO government* (No. 2/2008). University of Tasmania School of Accounting & Corporate Governance Working Paper Series. Retrieved from http://eprints.utas.edu.au/6193/1/OKeefeConwayForAuthorReview.pdf

Osma, B. G., & Guillamón-Saorín, E. (2009). Corporate governance and impression management in annual results press releases. *Accounting, Organizations and Society, 36*(4), 187–208.

Pandey, J. (1981). A note about social power through ingratiation among workers.

Journal of Occupational Psychology, 54(1), 65–67. doi:10.1111/j.2044-8325.1981.tb00044.x

Pang, B., & Lee, L. (2008). Opinion mining and sentiment analysis. *Foundations and Trends in Information Retrieval, 2*(1–2), 1–35. doi:10.1561/1500000011

Parhankangas, A., & Ehrlich, M. (2012). If you don't have anything nice to say, don't say anything at all: How blasting the competition affects your chances of raising business angel funding. *Frontiers of Entrepreneurship Research, 32*(1), 1.

Patelli, L., & Pedrini, M. (2013). Is the optimism in CEO's letters to shareholders sincere? Impression management versus communicative action during the economic crisis. *Journal of Business Ethics, 124*(1), 19–34. doi:10.1007/s10551-013-1855-3

Pollach, I., & Kerbler, E. (2011). Appearing competent: A study of impression management in U.S. and European CEO profiles. *Journal of Business Communication, 48*(4), 355–372. doi:10.1177/0021943611414687

Press, A. (2013, August 31). Study shows drop in demand for legal services. *The American Lawyer.*

Protection of Human Subjects Act, 45 C.F.R. § 46.101 (2009). Retrieved from http://www.hhs.gov/ohrp/policy/ohrpregulations.pdf

Rahman, S. (2012). Impression management motivations, strategies, and disclosure credibility of corporate narratives. *Journal of Management Research, 4*(3), 1–15. doi:10.5296/jmr.v4i3.1576

Rose, M. R., Diamond, S. S., & Baker, K. M. (2010). Goffman on the jury: Real juror's attention to the "offstage" of trials. *Law and Human Behavior, 34*(4), 310–323. doi:10.1007/s10979-009-9195-7

Saldana, J. (2009). *The coding manual for qualitative researchers.* Thousand Oaks, CA.Sage.

Saxton, G. D., & Guo, C. (2012, Dec. 18). Conceptualizing web-based stakeholder communication: The organizational website as a stakeholder relations tool. *Communication & Science Journal.*

Schau, H. J., Muniz Jr, A. M., & Arnould, E. J. (2009). How brand community practices create value. *Journal of Marketing,* 73(5), 30-51.

Schniederjans, D., Cao, E., & Schniederjans, M. (2013). Enhancing financial performance with social media: An impression management perspective. *Decision Support Systems,* 55(4), 911–918. doi:10.1016/j.dss.2012.12.027. Tetlock, P. C., Saar-Tsechanshy, M., & Macskassy, S. (2008). More than words: Quantifying language to measure firm's fundamentals. *The Journal of Finance,* 63(3), 1437–467.

Turnley, W., & Bolino, M. (2001). Achieving desired images while avoiding undesired images: Exploring the role of self-monitoring in impression management. *Journal of Applied Psychology* 2(86), 351–360. doi:10.1037//0021-9010.86.2.351

Tyler, J. M., Connaughton, S. L., Desrayaud, N., & Fedesco, H. N. (2012). Organizational impression management: Utilizing anticipatory tactics. *Basic and Applied Social Psychology*, *34*(4), 336–348. doi:10.1080/01973533.2012.693449

Vielhaber, M., & Waltman, J. (2008). Changing uses of technology: Crisis communication responses in a faculty strike. *Journal of Business Communication, 45*(3), 308–330. doi:10.1177/0021943608317112

Vinson, K. E. (2010). The blurred boundaries of social networking in the legal field: Just "face" it. *The University of Memphis Law Review, 2*(41), 355–412.

Vlasic, G., & Langer, J. (2012). Concept of reputation: Different perspectives and robust empirical understandings. *Trziste/Market, 24*(2), 219–244.

Ward, A., & Brenner, L. (2006). Accentuate the negative: The positive effects of negative acknowledgment. *Psychological Science, 17*(11), 959–962. doi:10.1111/j.1467- 9280.2006.01812.x

Westphal, J., Park, S., McDonald, M., & Hayward, M. (2012). Helping other CEOs avoid bad press: Social exchange and impression management support among CEOs in communications with journalists. *Administrative Science Quarterly, 57*(2), 217– 268. doi:10.1177/0001839212453267

Winter, S., Saunders, C., & Hart, P. (2003). Electronic window dressing: Impression management with websites. *European Journal of Information Systems, 12*(4), 309–322. doi:10.1057/palgrave.ejis.3000470

Yun, S., Takeuchi, R., & Liu, W. (2007). Employee self-enhancement motives and job performance behaviors: Investigating the moderating effects of employee role ambiguity and managerial perceptions of employee commitment. *Journal of Applied Psychology, 92*(3), 745–746. doi:10.1037/0021-9010.92.3.745

Yuthas, K., Rogers, R., & Dillard, J. F. (2002). Communicative action and corporate annual reports. *Journal of Business Ethics, 41*, 141–157.

Zavattaro, S. M. (2013). Expanding Goffman's theater metaphor to an identity-based view of place branding. *Administrative Theory & Praxis (M.E. Sharpe), 35*(4), 510–528. doi:10.2753/ATP1084-1806350403

Zeller, T., Stanko, B., & Jin, H. (2012). Investigating presentational change in company annual reports: An extension. *Accounting & Financial Studies Journal, 16*(3), 1–12.

Zhang, Y., & Wildemuth, B. M. (2009). Qualitative analysis of content. In B. Wildemuth (Ed.), *Applications of social research methods to questions in information and library science* (pp. 308–319). Westport, CT: Libraries Unlimited.

Zinko, R., Furner, C., Royle, T., & Hall, A. (2010). Self-perceptions of our personal reputations: The mediating role of image in the development of organizational citizenship behaviors. *Journal of International Management Studies, 5*(1), 1–9.

Appendix A. Data Analysis

Research Questions	Hypotheses	List of Variables	Instrument	Analysis Plan
R1: Do differences exist in any of the five OIM strategy metrics based on revenue (bottom quartile versus top quartile)?	H_1: At least one of the five OIM strategy metrics will be different based on revenue (bottom quartile versus top quartile). $H01$: None of the five OIM strategy metrics will be different based on revenue (bottom quartile versus top quartile).	Five Master Variables: Optimism (DV) Certainty (DV) Activity (DV) Realism (DV) Commonality (DV) Annual gross revenues (IV)	*American Lawyer* financial rankings 2013; Annual gross revenues Public data from organizational social media sites.	Descriptive and historical content analysis. Diction 7.0 (Hart, 2014) content analysis software for measurement of rhetorical tone; the Statistical Package for Social Sciences (SPSS) for comparative analysis, descriptive statistics, and hypotheses testing; repeated measures ANOVA.
R2: Do differences exist in any of the five OIM strategy metrics based on specialty (labor law versus intellectual property versus product liability)?	H_2: At least one of the five OIM strategy metrics will be different based on specialty (labor law versus intellectual property versus product liability). H_{02}: None of the five OIM strategy metrics will be different based on specialty (labor law versus intellectual property versus product liability).	Five Master Variables: Optimism (DV) Certainty (DV) Activity (DV) Realism (DV) Commonality (DV) Specialty type (IV)	*American Lawyer* financial rankings 2013; annual gross revenues Public data from organizational social media sites.	Descriptive and historical content analysis. Diction 7.0 (Hart, 2014) content analysis software for measurement of rhetorical tone; the Statistical Package for Social Sciences (SPSS) for comparative analysis, descriptive statistics, and hypotheses testing; repeated measures ANOVA.

Research Questions	Hypotheses	List of Variables	Instrument	Analysis Plan
R3: Do differences exist in any of the five OIM strategy metrics based on year (2010 through 2014)?	H_3: At least one of the five OIM strategy metrics will be different based on year (2010 through 2014). H_{03}: None of the five OIM strategy metrics will be different based on year (2010 through 2014).	Five Master Variables: Optimism (DV) Certainty (DV) Activity (DV) Realism (DV) Commonality (DV) Annual gross revenues (IV) Specialty type (IV)	*American Lawyer* financial rankings 2013; annual gross revenues. Public data from organizational social media sites.	Descriptive and historical content analysis. Diction 7.0 (Hart, 2014) content analysis software for measurement of rhetorical tone; the Statistical Package for Social Sciences (SPSS) for comparative analysis, descriptive statistics, and hypotheses testing; repeated measures ANOVA.

Appendix B. Methodology of OIM Studies

Study	Method	Analysis	Diction Software
Avery and McKay (2006)	Pictoral content analysis	Descriptive Analysis	X
Brennan et al. (2013)	Qualitative content analysis	Descriptive Analysis	
Chilcutt (2009)	Qualitative content analysis	Descriptive Analysis; Cross-tabulation, correlational associations	
Craig and Brennan (2012)	Quantitative content analysis	Descriptive Statistics, Multiple Regression, and Correlational Analysis	X
Craig et al. (2013)	Quantitative content analysis	Descriptive Analysis	X
Hall et al. (2013)	Qualitative content analysis	Descriptive Analysis	X
Huang et al. (2011)	Mixed methods content analysis	Chi-square tests Descriptive Statistics	
Lamertz and Martens (2011)	Mixed methods content analysis	Qualitative text coding; Correlational and Multiple Regression	
McDonnell and King (2013)	Quantitative content analysis	Causal-Correlational Paired t-tests Binomial Regression	
O'Keefe and Conway (2008)	Mixed methods content analysis	Mann-Whitney U score	
Osma and Guillamón-Saorín (2009)	Mixed methods content (textual) analysis	Multivariate Regression	

Study	Method	Analysis	Diction Software
Parhankangas and Ehrlich (2012)	Mixed methods content analysis	Descriptive Analysis; Linear Regression	X
Patelli and Pedrini (2013)	Quantitative content (textual) analysis	Regression Analysis	X
Pollach and Kerbler (2011)	Quantitative content analysis	Regression Analysis	
Schau, Muniz, and Arnould (2009)	Qualitative case study	Descriptive Analysis	
Schniederjans et al. (2013)	Quantitative content analysis	Automated text classification; Multiple Regression	X
Huang et al. (2011)	Mixed methods content analysis	Chi-square test for independence	
Tetlock et al. (2008)	Mixed methods content analysis	Descriptive Statistics, Multiple Regression, and Correlational Analysis	
Tyler et al. (2012)	Qualitative content analysis	Descriptive Analysis; ANOVA	
Vielhaber and Waltman (2008)	Qualitative case study	Descriptive Analysis	

Appendix C. Diction Variables

Master Variables Definition and Formula

Activity: Language featuring movement, change, the implementation of ideas, and the avoidance of inertia [Aggression + Accomplishment + Communication + Motion] − [Cognitive Terms + Passivity + Embellishment].

Optimism: Language endorsing some person, group, concept, or event or highlighting their positive entailments [Praise + Satisfaction + Inspiration] − [Blame + Hardship + Denial].

Certainty: Language indicating resoluteness, inflexibility, and completeness and a tendency to speak *ex cathedra* [Tenacity + Leveling + Collectives + Insistence] − [Numerical Terms + Ambivalence + Self- Reference + Variety].

Realism: Language describing tangible, immediate, recognizable matters that affect people's everyday lives [Familiarity + Spacial Awareness + Temporal Awareness + Present Concern + Human Interest + Concreteness] − [Past Concern + Complexity]. **Commonality:** Language highlighting the agreed-upon values of a group and rejecting idiosyncratic models of engagement [Centrality + Cooperation + Rapport] – [Diversity + Exclusion + Liberation].

Sub-variables

Numerical Terms: Any sum, date, or product specifying the facts in a given case. This dictionary treats each isolated integer and each separate group of integers as a single word. In addition, the dictionary contains common numbers in lexical format (e.g., one, tenfold, hundred, zero) as well as terms indicating numerical operations (e.g., subtract, divide, multiply, percentage) and quantitative topics (e.g., digitize, tally, mathematics). The presumption is that Numerical Terms hyper-specify a claim, thus detracting from its universality.

Ambivalence: Words expressing hesitation or uncertainty, implying a speaker's inability or unwillingness to commit to the verbalization being made. Included are hedges (e.g., allegedly, perhaps, might), statements of inexactness (e.g., almost, approximate, vague, somewhere), and confusion (e.g., baffled, puzzling, hesitate). Also included are words of restrained possibility (*could, would, he'd*) and mystery (*dilemma, guess, suppose, seems*). **Self-reference:** All first-person references, including *I, I'd, I'll, I'm,*

I've, me, mine, my, and *myself.* Self-references are treated as acts of indexing whereby the locus of action appears to reside in the speaker and not in the world at large, thereby implicitly acknowledging the speaker's limited vision.

Variety: This measure conforms to Johnson's (1946) Type-Token Ratio, which divides the number of different words in a passage by the passage's total words. A high score indicates a speaker's avoidance of overstatement and a preference for precise, molecular statements.

Tenacity: All uses of the verb *to be* (e.g., *is, am, will, shall*), three definitive verb forms (e.g., *has, must, do*), and their variants, as well as all associated contraction's (e.g., *he'll, they've, ain't*). These verbs connote confidence and totality.

Leveling Terms: Words used to ignore individual differences and to build a sense of completeness and assurance. Included are totalizing terms (e.g., *everybody, anyone, each, fully*), adverbs of permanence (e.g., *always, completely, inevitably, consistently*), and resolute adjectives (e.g., *unconditional, consummate, absolute, open-and-shut*).

Collectives: Singular nouns connoting plurality that function to decrease specificity. These words reflect a dependence on categorical modes of thought. Included are social groupings (e.g., *crowd*, *choir*, *team*, *humanity*), task groups (e.g., *army*, *congress*, *legislature*, *staff*), and geographical entities (e.g., *county*, *world*, *kingdom*, *republic*).

Insistence: A measure of code-restriction and semantic contentedness. The assumption is that repetition of key terms indicates a preference for a limited, ordered world. In calculating Insistence, all words occurring three or more times that function as nouns or noun-derived adjectives are identified (either cybernetically or by hand), and the following calculation performed: [Number of Eligible Words x Sum of their Occurrences] ÷ 10. For small input files, high-frequency terms used two or more times are used in the calculation.

Praise: Affirmations of some person, group, or abstract entity. Included are terms isolating important social qualities (e.g., *dear*, *delightful*, *witty*), physical qualities (e.g., *mighty*, *handsome*, *beautiful*), intellectual qualities (e.g., *shrewd*, *bright*, *vigilant*, *reasonable*), entrepreneurial qualities (e.g., *successful*, *conscientious*, *renowned*), and moral qualities (e.g., *faithful*, *good*, *noble*). All terms in this dictionary are adjectives. **Satisfaction:** Terms associated with positive affective states (e.g., *cheerful*, *passionate*, *happiness*), moments of undiminished joy (e.g., *thanks*, *smile*, *welcome*) and pleasurable diversion (*excited*, *fun*, *lucky*), or moments of triumph (e.g., *celebrating*, *pride*, *auspicious*). Also included are words of nurturance, such as *healing*, *encourage*, *secure*, and *relieved*.

Inspiration: Abstract virtues deserving of universal respect. Most of the terms in this dictionary are nouns isolating desirable moral qualities (e.g., *faith, honesty, self-sacrifice, virtue*) as well as attractive personal qualities (e.g., *courage, dedication, wisdom, mercy*). Social and political ideals are also included, such as *patriotism, success, education,* and *justice*.

Blame: Terms designating social inappropriateness (e.g., *mean, naive, sloppy, stupid*) as well as downright evil (e.g., *fascist, blood-thirsty, repugnant, malicious*). In addition, adjectives describing unfortunate circumstances (e.g., *bankrupt, rash, morbid, embarrassing*) or unplanned vicissitudes (e.g., *weary, nervous, painful, detrimental*) are included. The dictionary also contains outright denigrations, such as *cruel, illegitimate, offensive,* and *miserly*.

Hardship: Natural disasters (e.g., *earthquake, starvation, tornado, pollution*), hostile actions (e.g., *killers, bankruptcy, enemies, vices*), and censurable human behavior (e.g., *infidelity, despots, betrayal*). It also includes unsavory political outcomes (e.g., *injustice, slavery, exploitation, rebellion*) as well as normal human fears (e.g., *grief, unemployment, died, apprehension*) and incapacities (e.g., *error, cop-outs, weakness*).

Denial: A dictionary consisting of standard negative contractions (e.g., *aren't, shouldn't, don't*), negative functions words (e.g., *nor, not, nay*), and terms designating null sets (e.g., *nothing, nobody, none*).

Aggression: A dictionary embracing human competition and forceful action. Its terms connote physical energy (e.g., *blast, crash, explode, collide*), social domination (e.g., *conquest, attacking, dictatorships, violation*), and goal-directedness (e.g., *crusade, commanded, challenging, overcome*). In addition, words associated with personal triumph (e.g., *mastered, rambunctious, pushy*), excess human energy (e.g., *prod, poke, pound, shove*), disassembly (e.g., *dismantle, demolish, overturn, veto*), and resistance (e.g., *prevent, reduce, defend, curbed*) are included.

Accomplishment: Words expressing task-completion (e.g., *establish, finish, influence, proceed*) and organized human behavior (e.g., *motivated, influence, leader, manage*). Includes capitalistic terms (e.g., *buy, produce, employees, sell*), modes of expression (e.g., *grow, increase, generate, construction*), and general functionality (e.g., *handling, strengthen, succeed, outputs*). Also included is programmatic language, such as *agenda, enacted, working*, and *leadership*.

Communication: Terms referring to social interaction, both face-to-face (e.g., *listen, interview, read, speak*) and mediated (e.g., *film, videotape,* *telephone, e-mail).* The dictionary includes both modes of intercourse (e.g., *translate, quote, scripts, broadcast*) and moods of intercourse (e.g., *chat, declare, flatter, demand*). Other terms refer to social actors (e.g., *reporter, spokesperson, advocates, preacher*) and a variety of social purposes (e.g., *hint, rebuke, respond, persuade*).

Motion: Terms connoting human movement (e.g., *bustle, job, lurch, leap*), physical processes (e.g., *circulate, momentum, revolve, twist*), journeys (e.g., *barnstorm, jaunt, wandering, travels*), speed (e.g., *lickety-split, nimble, zip, whistle-stop*), and modes of transit (e.g., *ride, fly, glide, swim*).

Cognition: Words referring to cerebral processes, both functional and imaginative. Included are modes of discovery (e.g., *learn, deliberate, consider, compare*), domains of study (e.g., *biology, psychology, logic, economics*), mental challenges (e.g., *question, forget, re-examine, paradoxes*), institutional learning practices (e.g., *graduation, teaching, classrooms*), and three forms of intellection: intuitional (e.g., *invent, perceive, speculate, interpret*), rationalistic (e.g., *estimate, examine, reasonable, strategies*), and calculative (e.g., *diagnose, analyze, software, fact-finding*).

Passivity: Words ranging from neutrality to inactivity. Includes terms of compliance (e.g., *allow, tame, appeasement*), docility (e.g., *submit,* *contented, sluggish*), and cessation (e.g., *arrested, capitulate, refrain, yielding*). Also contains tokens of inertness (e.g., *backward, immobile, silence, inhibit*) and disinterest (e.g., *unconcerned, nonchalant, stoic*), as well as tranquility (e.g., *quietly, sleepy, vacation*).

Embellishment: A selective ratio of adjectives to verbs based on Boder's (1940) conception that heavy modification slows down a verbal passage by de-emphasizing human and material action. Embellishment is calculated according to the following formula: [Praise + Blame +1] ÷ [Present Concern + Past Concern +1].

Familiarity: Consists of a selected number of Ogden's (1968) operation words, which he calculates to be the most common words in the English language. Included are common prepositions (e.g., *across, over, through*), demonstrative pronouns (e.g., *this, that*) and interrogative pronouns (e.g., *who, what*), and a variety of particles, conjunctions, and connectives (e.g., *a, for, so*).

Spatial Terms: Terms referring to geographical entities, physical distances, and modes of measurement. Included are general geographical terms (e.g., *abroad, elbow-room, locale, outdoors*) as well as specific ones (e.g., *Ceylon, Kuwait, Poland*). Also included are politically defined locations (e.g., *county, fatherland, municipality, ward*), points on the compass (e.g., *east, southwest*) and the globe (e.g., *latitude, coastal, border, snowbelt*), as well as terms of scale (e.g., *kilometer, map, spacious*), quality (e.g., *vacant, out-of-the-way, disoriented*), and change (e.g., *pilgrimage, migrated, frontier.*)

Temporal Terms: Terms that fix a person, idea, or event within a specific time interval, thereby signaling a concern for concrete and practical matters. The dictionary designates literal time (e.g., *century, instant, mid-morning*) as well as metaphorical designations (e.g., *lingering, seniority, nowadays*). Also included are calendrical terms (e.g., *autumn, year-round, weekend*), elliptical terms (e.g., *spontaneously, postpone, transitional*), and judgmental terms (e.g., *premature, obsolete, punctual*).

Present Concern: A selective list of present tense verbs extrapolated from Ogden's list of general and picturable terms, all of which occur with great frequency in standard American English. The dictionary is not topic-specific but points instead to general physical activity (e.g., *cough, taste, sing, take*), social operations (e.g., *canvass, touch, govern, meet*), and task-performance (e.g., *make, cook, print, paint*).

Human Interest: An adaptation of Flesch's (1951) notion that concentrating on people and their activities gives discourse a life-like quality. Included are standard personal pronouns (e.g., *he, his, ourselves, them*), family members and relations (e.g., *cousin, wife, grandchild, uncle*), and generic terms (e.g., *friend, baby, human, persons*).

Concreteness: A large dictionary possessing no thematic unity other than tangibility and materiality. Included are sociological units (e.g., *peasants, African-Americans, Catholics*), occupational groups (e.g., *carpenter, manufacturer, policewoman*), and political alignments (e.g., *Communists, congressman, Europeans*). Also incorporated are physical structures (e.g., *courthouse, temple, store*), forms of diversion (e.g., *television, football, CD-ROM*), terms of accountancy (e.g., *mortgage, wages, finances*), and modes of transportation (e.g., *airplane, ship, bicycle*). In addition, the dictionary includes body parts (e.g., *stomach, eyes, lips*), articles of clothing (e.g., *slacks, pants, shirt*), household animals (e.g., *cat, insects, horse*) and foodstuffs (e.g., *wine, grain, sugar*), and general elements of nature (e.g., *oil, silk, sand*).

Past Concern: The past-tense forms of the verbs in the present concern category.

Complexity: A simple measure of the average number of characters-per-word in a given input file. Borrows Flesch's (1951) notion that convoluted phrasings make a text's ideas abstract and its implications unclear.

Centrality: Terms denoting institutional regularities and/or substantive agreement on core values. Included are indigenous terms (e.g., *native, basic, innate*) and designations of legitimacy (e.g., *orthodox, decorum, constitutional, ratified*), systematicity (e.g., *paradigm, bureaucratic, ritualistic*), and typicality (e.g., *standardized, matter-of-fact, regularity*). Also included are terms of congruence (e.g., *conformity, mandate, unanimous*), predictability (e.g., *expected, continuity, reliable*), and universality (e.g., *womankind, perennial, landmarks*).

Rapport: Included are terms of affinity (e.g., *congenial, camaraderie, companion*), assent (e.g., *approve, vouched, warrants*), deference (e.g., *tolerant, willing, permission*), and id entity (e.g., *equivalent, resemble, consensus*).

Cooperation: Terms designating behavioral interactions among people that often result in a group product. Included are designations of formal work relations (e.g., *unions, schoolmates, caucus*) and informal associations (e.g., *chum, partner, cronies*) to more intimate interactions (e.g., *sisterhood, friendship, comrade*). Also included are neutral interactions (e.g., *consolidate, mediate, alignment*), job-related tasks (e.g., *network, detente, exchange*), personal involvement (e.g., *teamwork, sharing, contribute*), and self- denial (e.g., *public-spirited, care-taking, self-sacrifice*).

Diversity: Words describing individuals or groups of individuals differing from the norm. Such distinctiveness may be comparatively neutral (e.g., *inconsistent, contrasting,* non-*conformist*) but can also be positive (e.g., *exceptional, unique, individualistic*) or negative (e.g., *illegitimate, rabble-rouser, extremist*). Functionally, heterogeneity may be an asset (e.g., *far-flung, dispersed, diffuse*) or a liability (e.g., *factionalism, deviancy, quirky*) as can its characterizations: rare vs. Queer, variety vs. Jumble, distinctive vs. Disobedient.

Exclusion: A dictionary describing the sources and effects of social isolation. Such seclusion can be phrased passively (e.g., *displaced, sequestered*), positively (e.g., *self- contained, self-sufficient*), or negatively (e.g., *outlaws, repudiated*). Moreover, it can result from voluntary forces (e.g., *secede, privacy*) and involuntary forces (e.g., *ostracize, forsake, discriminate*) and from both personality factors (e.g., *smallmindedness, loneliness*) and political factors (e.g., *right-wingers, nihilism*). Exclusion is often a dialectical concept: hermit vs. Derelict, refugee vs. Pariah, discard vs. Spurn.

Liberation: Terms describing the maximizing of individual choice (e.g., *autonomous, open-minded, options*) and the rejection of social conventions (e.g., *unencumbered, radical, released*). Liberation is motivated by both personality factors (e.g., *eccentric, impetuous, flighty*) and political forces (e.g., *suffrage, liberty, freedom, emancipation*) and may produce dramatic outcomes (e.g., *exodus, riotous, deliverance*) or subdued effects (*loosen, disentangle, outpouring*). Liberatory terms also admit to rival characterizations: exemption vs. Loophole, elope vs. Abscond, uninhibited vs. Outlandish.

Appendix D. OIM tied to Rhetorical Tone Variables

Study	Variable	OIM category	Finding
Craig and Brennan (2012)	Realism Master Variable	Direct Assertive OIM behaviors	Realism used to study reputation; high reputation firms scored higher on this variable representative of tangible, immediate concerns of everyday life.
Craig et al. (2013)	Certainty Master Variable	Direct Assertive OIM behaviors	Certainty used to measure deceptive content in corporate letters. Results found high uncertainty (low certainty) is associated with a high probability of deception.
Craig et al. (2013); Vielhaber and Waltman (2008)	Diction sub-variable Numerical terms	OIM defensive behaviors	Negative tone, use of personal pronouns; Diction numerical terms - inclusion (or exclusion) of quantitative information in company narratives as a way of managing external perceptions.
Lamertz and Martens (2011)	Commonality Master Variable	Indirect Assertive	Association on professional firms and an IPO network helps construct organizational image and impression management bases on Goffman's team efforts to control a situation.
McDonnell and King (2013)	Did not use Diction Claims of activity, diversity, pro-social claims	Indirect Defensive OIM categorical behaviors	Philanthropy and claims of social responsibility; buffering-using prosocial claims to neutralize threat and refereeing - reliance on past prosocial claims to offset future threat.
Parhankangas and Ehrlich (2012)	Diction sub-variables Blame, denial, justification, apology	Indirect Defensive	Focus on negative words and sub-variables in Diction.

Study	Variable	OIM category	Finding
Patelli and Pedrini (2013)	Diction sub-variables Blame, denial, justification, apology	Indirect Defensive	Optimism linked to sincerity; emphasis on positive information while obfuscating negative information; Tone of CEO letters / Optimism is a statistically significant predictor of future performance.
Patelli and Pedrini (2013)	Commonality Master Variable	Indirect Assertive	Found that non-engaging language (low commonality) associated with lower performance.
Pollach and Kerbler (2011)	Did not use Diction	Assertive OIM categorical behaviors	Philanthropy and claims of social responsibility.
Schniederjans et al. (2013)	Diction sub-variables apology, justification	Direct Assertive/ Indirect Defensive strategies	Defensive/proactive strategies to defend image.
Tetlock et al. (2008)	Did not use Diction	Direct Defensive strategies	Negative words in financial press often forecast low firm earnings and are predictors of returns and stock market prices.
Vielhaber and Waltman (2008)	Diction sub-variables denial, justification	Indirect Defensive OIM strategies	Include attacking the accuser, denial, excuses, justification, ingratiation – strategies to counter negativity, praise a stakeholder, or remind public of good deeds to maintain legitimacy and reputation.

Appendix E. Research in Motion

Introduction to RIM

Research in Motion (RIM) was founded in 1984. The company resides in Waterloo, Canada but has several offices in Asia-Pacific, Europe and the US. RIM has become a global leader within wireless technology and today exports smartphones, tablets and software. Its most popular product to date, the BlackBerry, was launched in

1999 and is used by millions today (RIM – Company, 2012). The company has always benefited from being known as an innovative front-runner within its field and in many countries its products were savored by enterprise users over competitors in the likes of Apple and Samsung. A decline in sales has however started to show as competition intensifies and RIM's core capacities no longer offer a solution the majority of consumers are interested in (Gasseé, April 2, 2012). Combined with experiencing various crises and issues, this is a tough period in the history of the Canadian company. The assessment of how the October Outage was handled should not be carried out without having looked at RIM as an organization.

As mentioned earlier Research in Motion is a relatively young company, its history going back to the mid-eighties. The BlackBerry solution, which the crisis is connected to, was not introduced until 1999. Noteworthy of RIM, is that it is a company selling innovative, wireless solutions and therefore deals with complicated technology on a daily basis. Furthermore, the company operates within the ever-evolving mobile industry and it can therefore be assumed that RIM has to stay on top of the newest media trends in order to compete with other competitors. In other words, RIM is a tech savvy brand that is no stranger to social media, as they have to come up with new media solutions for the BlackBerry continuously. Also, judging from activity on RIM's own accounts, the company has incorporated social media largely into its communication with stakeholders (the BlackBerry Youtube page e.g. features over 1400 posted videos since its creation in 2006). Based on this characteristic alone, RIM ought to navigate a crisis within an online platform well. Nonetheless, being tech savvy does not equal being able to handle a crisis successfully.

The crisis history of RIM

RIM is a fairly "young" company, therefore its history of crises is not that deep. However, being a company within the wireless mobile industry RIM has experienced sharp competition from other tech brands and being constantly pressured to withhold its global leader status RIM naturally has experienced complications. Firstly, RIM has been involved in lawsuits regarding patent litigation numerous times. For the most part, the company has filed suits against competitors who have apparently infringed on patents.

On January 22, 2010 Motorola filed a lawsuit against Blackberry for five infringements of patent. This caused a long conflict, which was finally settled on June 11, 2010 (Patel, 2010, January 22). RIM was involved in another crisis that occurred shortly after the October Outage, when Vodafone users started experiencing how their prepaid balances were getting deducted or reduced without any usage. Vodafone was deemed the culprit in this case but unfortunately it also rubbed of on RIM (Bafna, 2011, December 9). The company has also experienced several service failures, one of them happening in September 2011, where the BlackBerry Messenger service went down for several hours in Canada and Latin America. Outages have also occurred frequently, some of the most recent in dominant markets such as South Africa and the UK (Austen, 2011, October 11). Finally, the crisis with by far the most impact was the four-day network outage in October 2011, which this thesis will analyze. The outage was a result of a technological error, but happened entirely under the auspices of RIM. Therefore, in the company's history of crises, this must be categorized as one of the more grave, if not the worst.

The October Outage

During October 2011, RIM faced one of its most challenging crises so far. Users of the very popular Smartphone, BlackBerry, began to experience messaging and browsing delays, which evolved into a full on network collapse apparently caused by "a core switch failure within RIM's infrastructure" (BlackBerry, 2011, October 11th). The outage spread through Europe, the Middle East, Africa, India and parts of South America. Judging by user posts on Blackberry's Facebook page the first signal interruptions began around 10 am on October 10th and lasted until the evening on October 13th. The first update from RIM was posted on Twitter on October 10th at 4.11 pm followed by a notification on Facebook almost ten hours later at 01.48 am. The Youtube video featuring a message from CEO of RIM, Mike Lazaridis, was not publicized until October 13th. Interestingly, RIM chose not to issue a press release on the company website, however they did create the "BlackBerry Service Update" page on which short updates from the company were uploaded. These communicative efforts, along with a press conference carried out on October 12th, constituted the part of RIM's crisis response effort that will be analyzed below.

Analysis of RIM's crisis strategy

Introduction to RIM's social media strategy

As mentioned earlier, RIM's Twitter account will not be analyzed due to space limitations but it seems necessary to note that this was in fact the first medium to communicate the crisis to the public (Research In Motion, 2011, October 10 4.11pm). Also, this was the medium where BlackBerry users began a long stream of complaints. The first user generated post on Facebook concerning the crisis was posted on October 12th by Hyacinth Sintiago and was entitled "how to survive the blackberry meltdown!" (2011, October 12, 11.05pm). It could be assumed that other users may have contacted RIM via the Facebook chat or message applications but otherwise, until then, they had expressed their frustration by commenting on the posts authored by RIM. The first of these was, as aforementioned, posted the day before and was followed by two consecutive posts as well as several more over the following days as the crisis developed. Another substantial part of RIM's crisis strategy was a Youtube video, which to date has reached close to 400.000 views. The video shows RIM's CEO, Mike Lazaridis, addressing stakeholders with a message on behalf of the company and him (BlackBerry, 2011, October 13). The video wasn't released until two days after the crisis started. It was then spread virally through Twitter, Facebook and the company website as a hyperlink at the end of a message. Before beginning the analysis of RIM's social media response strategy the thesis will examine how the news media perceived and framed the company and situation in order to make an assessment of the aforementioned concept attribution of responsibility.

The news media response

When the BlackBerry crisis broke out news media worldwide were not late to comment on it. Two of the newspapers covering the crisis closely were

English The Guardian and American The New York Times. Both also run globally read digital newspapers online, from where the quotes mentioned in this paragraph stem. The Guardian released the first online article about the network outage on the 10th of October describing the situation and crisis under way. The NY Time's article followed on October 11th and could report about how far the crisis had spread and what RIM's response had been. Especially the article from The Guardian portrays RIM through a negative angle stating, "The failure will be a huge embarrassment for the company" and pulling out the employee quote "The attitude was, 'We're going to grow and grow but making sure our infrastructure can support it isn't a priority.' (Arthur, 2011, October 10). In an article following up on the restoration of services the missing rights of the stakeholders were also emphasized: "Consumers are apparently excluded from any guarantee of service by a clause in RIM's terms and conditions" (Arthur, 2011, October 13). What can be drawn from these quotes is that the newspaper frames RIM as a rather irresponsible company that is more interested in growth than delivering reliable and guaranteed service to its stakeholders. The first article also insinuates that the company has been too slow to react to the crisis through the quote that the outage "was still affecting users more than four hours later with no time given for when it was expected to be resolved." (Arthur, 2011, October 10).

This suggests evidence that The Guardian attributes the responsibility entirely to RIM and deems the company the villain. Less blatant is the framing in The NY Times. One of the reasons for this could be the fact that The US was not affected by the crisis and therefore the American media did not feel the need to lash out. The paper does however treat the subject critically. The first article includes quotes such as "many people seemed to be frustrated by the lack of communication from Research in Motion" and also a negative quote from a stakeholder about RIM being "Arrogant and disrespectful to its customers." (Austen, 2011, October 11). These quotes, when juxtaposed against sources from the Guardian, also give an impression of RIM being attributed responsibility. Furthermore, the perceived neglecting of stakeholders is also visible through the article. These are some of the similarities. Nevertheless, when examining articles written later, The NY Times frames RIM much less harshly, seemingly exercising a form of the aforesaid concept victimage. This can be seen from the following quotes: "Wednesday's hit could not have come at a worse time for RIM, which is fending off a growing crowd of agitated investors", "It's a bloodbath" (Wortham, 2011, October 12). This does not automatically prove that The NY Times was attributing blame away from RIM but it is indicative of a more nuanced framing than The Guardian. To sum up, despite different angles both mediums seem to have attributed more or less full responsibility to RIM.

The following paragraph will map out exactly what was communicated and how it was done i.e. the rhetorical strategy and then juxtapose these findings with the theory as put forth in the literature review, hopefully providing an answer to the problem statement.

Characterizing the crisis

In order to analyze RIM's response strategy it is necessary to look at the crisis situation and determine which type the company was dealing with. Very first it seems natural to determine whether or not the case should in fact be treated as a crisis in order to proceed with the analysis. The difference between crisis and issue essentially came down to the amount of damage caused and whether or not the entire organization was affected (Coombs, 1999). Externally, a Facebook quote posted by RIM summing up how wide spread the network outage was points towards the situation being more than a mere issue (BlackBerry, 2011, October 11, 10.34pm). Apart from the US, some of RIM's largest markets were stricken. In some of the countries affected, such as South Africa, the BlackBerry is the most dominant smart phone and the outage therefore caused a serious communication breach qua the large amount of stakeholders (Vermeulen, 2011, November 16).

Internally, the online effort of the company indicates that the situation had indeed disrupted the entire organization. If the problem had limited itself to e.g. one or two local areas, only regional departments might be affected due to proximity, hence probably only using regional Facebook pages and issuing messages from local managers. Instead, the international Facebook page was chosen as a tool, and a message was delivered globally from the top leader of the organization.

Now that the situation can be categorized as a crisis with some certainty, the next step is also to determine the crisis type through Coomb's and Benoit's theory. According to Coombs there were four crisis types each further categorized by intentionality and whether the crisis figured internally or externally. When taking these axes into account the October Outage can be viewed as an accident, seeing as the crisis happened internally and, judging from organizational and media quotes, was not intentional (e.g. BlackBerry, 2011, October 11, 10.34pm; Arthur, 2011, October 13). The initial problem was assigned a malfunctioned fail-over after a core switch failure in the network system (BlackBerry, October 11th, 10.34pm), and therefore, essentially, not a human error. However, the phrase "did not function as previously tested." from the same post shows that employees had been testing the system and therefore humans were involved in the process. It could even be assumed that they might have been able to predict the failure. This leads us to Benoit's perceptual wrongdoings. He also distinguishes between four different kinds. Common to all of them is that they are assigned human flaws. The fact that humans were engaged in the RIM crisis process is the instance that justifies applying Benoit's theory to the crisis. In the case of BlackBerry, the malfunction was technical but the system, in which it occurred, was monitored by humans and therefore the possibility that an employee could have predicted and intervened in the situation cannot be excluded. The type of wrongdoing that fits the situation most evolves around the environment surrounding the accused. Benoit claims that certain people, events etc. can prevent the accused from fulfilling responsibility. In this case the responsibility can be equated with the goal Lazaridis mentions in his Youtube speech and goes on to say that the goal was not delivered on during the crisis (appendix 1).

The accused could arguably be both the employees in charge of the network system or the company as a whole. RIM avoids scapegoating internally; therefore it can be assumed that RIM as a collective of people takes the blame. Finally, the event disrupting daily order, and creating the perceived wrongdoing, is of course the malfunctioned fail-over.

Before elaborating on and categorizing the response strategy it is necessary to further examine the attribution of responsibility and provide a picture of how the crisis was perceived and portrayed externally.

The various media quotes throughout the thesis have pointed towards both stakeholders and the news media primarily attributing responsibility to RIM. This is important knowledge when beginning to assess the company's response strategy, one of the reasons being that a main criterion of SCCT is the assessment of organizational responsibility. The theory posits that the degree of attributed responsibility by stakeholders determines the appropriate response to the crisis (Coombs, 2007).

Taking this statement as a point of departure, the best match of strategy for RIM would be acceptance of responsibility for the crisis. With this knowledge, certain strategies can be deemed more risky and difficult to carry out than others. Many organizations unfortunately manage to mismatch a strategy to their current crisis situation despite this, causing even more damage than anticipated (Benoit, 2007). In this case two of the strategies can be judged as hazardous for RIM. Firstly, the denial strategy would have been difficult to use, seeing as the public had already judged the situation and RIM would have a hard time persuading them to reconsider their judgment. Secondly, an attack strategy would also have been a misplaced response given the circumstances. This does however not automatically indicate that the

company refrained from using the two strategies. The following analysis will shed light on how RIM chose to handle the response strategy.

Rhetorical analysis of RIM's response strategy on Facebook

The preliminary strategy

The very first message delivered on Facebook began with the following sentence "We are pleased to report that BlackBerry email services have been restored." and was concluded in this way "We apologize to our customers for any inconvenience and we'll continue to update you as new information becomes available." (BlackBerry, 2011, October 11, 01.48am). This initial statement can, in accordance to Benoit, be categorized as an apologetic strategy that includes corrective action taken by the company. According to Pace et al, the apology lets the stakeholders know that the company feels guilty and understands the frustration over the error (2010). At first glance this could seem to be a sufficient solution, seeing as the crisis was deemed an internal and technical fault that RIM maybe could have predicted.

The company therefore shows remorse and begins to restore conditions. Despite this, at least two things might be problematic with this initial restoration strategy. Firstly, RIM made the mistake of proclaiming that the crisis was nearly over, when in fact, at the time, it had just began to gather strength. This move, paired with the previous quote, could be recognized as arrogant and be an expression of RIM not being in keeping with the situation. Secondly, an apology is not regarded by all as a means of taking full responsibility for an error, some merely view it as a way of expressing regret (Pace et al, 2010). This can be problematic if stakeholders expect RIM to voice an explicit acceptance of responsibility.

The next message delivered at 5.36pm goes on to inform that some users across the globe are still experiencing network delays followed by a lengthier message at 10.34pm stating that the delays "were caused by a core switch failure within RIM's infrastructure. Although the system is designed to failover to a back-up switch, the failover did not function as previously tested." (BlackBerry, 2011, October 11, 01.48am). These posts can be categorized as account strategies in which RIM seeks to explain the progress of the crisis, however, they also contain a degree of evasion of responsibility. The use of passive voice in the quote suggests evidence to this claim, as it can be used to conceal the doer of an action (Rosenwasser & Stephen, 2012). At no point does the subject (RIM) perform the action but is rather acted upon. This could indicate that the company has tried to disguise what is actually an excuse, as a simple informative account. Another noteworthy feature about the initial communication is that the first four posts have a variant of the sentence "we apologize for the inconvenience caused" in them. This points to RIM having assessed the apology to be an important part of the company's image restoration.

As the crisis deepens

After the first 24 hours of the crisis RIM seems to have realized that the problem is bigger than initially expected. This can e.g. be seen from the first message posted on Facebook on October 12th "We're aware many BlackBerry customers are experiencing intermittent service delays. Restoring full service is our number one priority" (BlackBerry, 2011, October 12, 4.45pm). It is probable that this message serves as an answer to the many angry comments made by stakeholders the day before. At the end of the message RIM provides a hyperlink to a "service update" page, which the company has chosen to create as an extra monitoring service. The link is shared on Facebook both on the 12th and 13th of October. Apart from this, the company's communicative efforts begin to shift focus in the postings on its Facebook page. Where each message earlier contained an apology, they begin to contain a "thank you" to the stakeholders together with updated accounts of the crisis progress. Thanking can be placed in the same category as apologizing, as both actions are expressions of mortification. Hereby RIM humbles itself and can hope for forgiveness (Benoit, 1997). This strategy provides no active explanation or justification and in RIM's case the frustration of the stakeholders begins to grow as an effect. Judging from many of their comments, they are feelings overlooked and their need for information disparaged: "Wow, 1 day fair enough, 2 days mildly annoying, 3, ridiculous, sort it out!" (Joe Thompson, 2011, October 13, 12.36am), "I like the way you just completely ignore all your customer's comments and just palm us off with a half hearted attempt at an apology!'' (Sean Eaton, 2011, October 13, 1.15am).

RIM chose not to answer any of the threads and comments made by its stakeholders, which could point towards the company having chosen a generic and less personal strategy. This choice has consequences as seen in the quotes above. Naturally, it is understandable that the company may have difficulty in answering thousands of comments each day, nevertheless several sources stress "that openness, transparency, and two-way communication are key element of successful crisis managements'' and therefore that rendering sincere, individualized communication can reduce the wrongdoing and cultivate a sense of understanding (Wigley&Zhang, 2011, p. 5; Macnamara, 2010). Two-way communication was also emphasized as one of the beneficial possibilities earlier when utilizing social media in crisis communication, and it can therefore seem puzzling why RIM, in the crisis situation, did not take more advantage of this tool.

Restoring conditions

October 13th 6.46pm RIM once again announces on Facebook that full service has been restored followed by a lengthier message thanking stakeholders for their patience. The mortification strategy continues as a red thread in the company's communication to the stakeholders. This time the problem has in fact been solved and RIM can begin restoring conditions to their previous state. The second message posted that day contains a link enabling users of the BlackBerry to confirm that they once again are able to receive emails. This can be analyzed as an attempt at further corrective action. Finally, RIM refers to a Twitter account for further help (BlackBerry, 2011, October 14, 4.31pm).

The final message on Facebook solely regarding the crisis is posted on October 17th. This message can be seen as an attempt to make amends. RIM is aware of the fact that its stakeholders are angry and feel as if something has been wrongfully taken from them the previous week, which needs to be compensated. "To show our appreciation, BlackBerry subscribers will receive a selection of premium apps (worth a total value of more than US $100) free of charge from BlackBerry App World" (BlackBerry, 2011, October 17, 10.35am). This response strategy was not touched upon in the literary review but is mentioned in the SCCT as simply a "compensation strategy". The strategy serves, like the apology, as a positive, rebuilding strategy and can ideally be used by companies in accidental crises coupled with crisis history (Coombs, 2007). Thus, theory supports RIM's choice to reimburse customers at the end of the crisis.

Rhetorical analysis of RIM's response strategy on Youtube

As mentioned in the introduction to RIM's social media strategy the company also chose to publish a video on Youtube showing CEO Mike Lazaridis presenting a speech directed at the stakeholders affected during the crisis. Before delving into the content of the speech, it seems necessary firstly to analyze what significance including this medium and message altogether did have for the response strategy.

A study put forth by Wright and Hinson examined the actual importance attributed various social media in PR together with the importance they ought to be attributed. The study showed that both Youtube and Facebook generally were less recognized conduits than they ought to be (as seen in Macnamara, 2010). This claim could indicate that RIM made a wise choice when employing these media, although the actual outcome of course rests on the content of the strategy also. In terms of combining Facebook and Youtube, there can be obvious complementing benefits by being able to utilize both a medium allowing immediate, two-way written communication and one allowing video and audio content. RIM must have considered this yet somehow did not provide the communicative content stakeholders expected. This claim will be elaborated on in the following paragraph.

In the speech Lazaridis begins by quoting RIM's main goal throughout the years of delivering "reliable real-time communications around the world" with emphasis on the word "reliable". He follows up by admitting that they "did not deliver on that goal this week. Not even close." (Appendix 1). This is the first time RIM actively admits to having failed to deliver what stakeholders expected. Although this is not an explicit expression of taking responsibility for the crisis, it does show that RIM feels responsible for failing to deliver its service as promised. The initial statement is followed by a personal apology from Lazaridis: "I apologise for the service outages this week. We've let many of you down." (Appendix 1). This leads back to the mortification strategy initially identified in the Facebook messages. RIM continues to humble itself towards the stakeholders. The next few sentences provide an account of what RIM is doing to fix the problem. Again, this is a strategy that the company also employed on Facebook, although the account is longer and more descriptive in the Youtube video. The next noteworthy sentence addresses the problem regarding lack of communication: "We know that you want to hear more from us, and we're working to update you more frequently through our websites and social media channels". Hereby RIM answers to the news media and stakeholders, who have accused the company of slow and insufficient communication to the public. Unfortunately, this message was not delivered until the final day of the network outage, which was probably too late to redeem any sort of goodwill. The idea of addressing the demands of the stakeholders is a reasonable one given e.g Benoit's rationale for restoring a reputation, stating, "perceptions are more important than reality" (1997, p. 178). In other words that RIM should strive to satisfy stakeholders regardless of what the company makes of its own strategy. If they point to a problem, RIM should address it, as they did in the sentence described above. The drawback in this case being that the message should have been delivered when it was essentially still relevant, rather than on the day the crisis was pronounced resolved.

The final part of the speech is a plea to the stakeholders to restore their trust in the company and have confidence in the fact that RIM are doing whatever possible to restore previous conditions. Lazaridis finishes with a "thank you" (appendix 1). This section also bears resemblance to some of the messages posted on Facebook by the company. The fact that the Youtube message to such a high degree echoes what has already been communicated on Facebook can both be seen as an advantage and a drawback. The advantage lies in consistency. Showing consistency in crisis communication can be an important way to build credibility. Inconsistency exhibits the organization's incompetency with crisis management (Coombs, 2010). However, as mentioned earlier, failing to meet expectations can also cause increased damage to a company's reputation. The drawback being that stakeholders presumably were expecting something more than what had already been communicated on Facebook, when RIM decided to use an entirely new medium featuring the CEO.

When evaluating the speech as a whole it is relevant to study what has been included and what has been omitted. As in the Facebook messages there once again is given an apology and once again there is an account of what the company is now reactively doing. One thing that has been omitted is the account of how the crisis happened, i.e. what went wrong. And still there is no mention of responsibility. RIM comes closer in the video by using active sentences instead of passive, and having either Lazaridis or the company as the main actor in the message, but an explicit expression of fault is never given. In this video RIM focuses entirely on the repercussions and resolving of the crisis. The message can be categorized as an extension of what was

already being posted on Facebook but with a more personal angle qua having Lazaridis be the spokesperson and drawing advantage of non-linguistic tools such as facial expressions and tone of voice. The same reputational rebuild strategies were used in both mediums in the form of apology, thanking and accounts.

Discussion

The primary purpose of this thesis was to examine how companies navigate crises in an online world, taking departure in the RIM crisis. Consistent with prior research within the field of social media and crisis communication, the results of the case study indicate that immediacy and elimination of geographical barriers have had an effect on how crises are handled. Stakeholders expect immediate response and a higher degree of coverage from a company involved in a crisis being communicated online. In keeping with the SCCT framework, the stakeholder assessment of responsibility is still vital for companies when designing a crisis response. Now more than ever it seems important to communicate responsibility. The findings illustrate that RIM was too late in responding and when the company finally did, the response was marked with vagueness in terms of who was to blame and when the crisis would actually be solved. Pace et al suggested that issuing an apology not necessarily lead to the perception that an organization was taking blame for a crisis. Instead, explicitly voicing acceptance of responsibility could lead to greater reputational protection (2010).

RIM chose not to do the latter and suffered reputational damage among stakeholders and the news media as an effect. A reason for acting as they did could be the fact that accepting responsibility is more costly than apologizing, with possible lawsuits in the offing. Perhaps RIM had hoped that offering a simple apology would have sufficed, as it does in some cases. Unfortunately for them, many stakeholders were not convinced by this approach. A recommendation for the company might be in the future to continuously use a response where accommodative and compensating strategies are still used but instead utilize the apology more carefully, hopefully framing it more sincerely. Also, focus could be on constructing messages with active sentences rather than passive, of course depending on the degree of responsibility assigned to RIM in future crises. Nevertheless, research points to the active voice being more transparent and credible than the passive, indicating that this would be the wise choice when attempting to conduct honest crisis communication (Rosenwasser & Stephen, 2012). When comparing this factor with the aforementioned critique of messages on social media lacking credibility, active rhetoric also seems to be a valid approach. An entirely different response strategy that RIM could have chosen to use is the excuse. The company's strategy for the October outage did have elements from this response strategy but it could have been carried out more consistently. RIM might then have denied the intent to do harm and claimed incapacity to control the events that triggered the crisis. If stakeholders where lead to believe this claim, it would minimize the organizational responsibility (Coombs, 2007).

An essential constituent of crisis communication theory was the history of crises, the so-called Velcro effect. In RIM a history of network outages was determined, having caused crisis-like situations previously and with probability eroding the stakeholder's confidence in the brand. Also, a number of other issues in the history of the company were described. It seems probable that this crisis history has affected how the October outage was perceived. In coherence with theory this crisis posed a large threat to the reputation of RIM and judging from the framing in the news media and response from stakeholders it was a matter of time before the network incidents developed into a full-blown crisis. This continuous string of problems could also be one of the explanations for the anger and frustration visible in customer comments. Since this was not an isolated crisis people had expected more from the company in terms of ready information about the situation and perhaps that RIM had been better prepared for the outage. In future crises the company should make sure to take its crisis history into account when designing a response strategy.

Conclusion

Currently, more and more research is showing the potential social media have to become a vital tool in crisis communication. Interestingly, this has still not motivated many companies to avail them of these new conduits. And many of those that have, fail to use them in a way that ends up contributing to a successful crisis strategy. Naturally, a lot more scholarly research needs to be conducted on the field, before the mechanics of social media are fully understood (this might not even be possible), however, studies for a company such as RIM to gain knowledge about how they should be communicating online do exist.

The findings of this thesis show that there is still some way to be covered before RIM grasps the consequences of utilizing social media. Theory shows that it can be a powerful instrument but only when used efficiently. For RIM the challenge, among other things, lies in combining ideas from the SCCT framework, crisis communication theory and response strategies with the advantageous traits of social media. Especially the factor of immediacy needs to be taken more seriously. It is no longer sufficient for a company to follow up on a crisis several hours after the outbreak. Online communication should be monitored closely and when a problem occurs stakeholders ought to be provided with a message instantly. This does not mean that weight not longer should be put on content of crisis communication, merely that the progress of the communication effort could be designed differently.

Future research should continue to examine the traits of social media and how they might be beneficial in a crisis communication context. The tools provided with this new technology are still relatively unexplored. With a better understanding of the technology crisis strategies could be tailored to be more efficient and precise. It could also be relevant to explore further how companies draw more advantage of two-way communication. Whether communication could be made more proficient and individually directed.

Also, research should study further the accommodative reputational response strategies and investigate whether expressions of responsibility could and ought to be utilized more and whether it would have an effect on the success of a strategy. Finally, theory on how organizations navigate online ought still to be extended. Possibly exploring the ideas of Crisisblogger further and providing a scholarly discussion of social media as an ever evolving concept, and if it can even be boxed and categorized as till now.

Lightning Source UK Ltd.
Milton Keynes UK
UKHW011312260220
359369UK00002B/370